D0166774

CHARLES M. NORTH & BOB SMIETANA

GOOD

INTENTIONS

CHARLES M. NORTH & BOB SMIETANA

GOOD INTENTIONS

Nine Hot-Button Issues Viewed
Through the Eyes of Faith

MOODY PUBLISHERS
CHICAGO

All Scripture quotations are taken from the *Holy Bible, New International Version* ®. NIV®. Copyright © 1973, 1978, 1984 by International Bible Society. Used by permission of Zondervan. All rights reserved.

Scripture quotations marked KJV are taken from the King James Version.

Scripture quotations marked ESV are taken from *The Holy Bible, English Standard Version*. Copyright © 2000, 2001 by Crossway Bibles, a division of Good News Publishers. Used by permission. All rights reserved.

Editor: Bobby Maddex
Interior Design: Ragont Design
Cover Design: Kirk Douponce, DogEared Design (www.DogEaredDesign.com)
Cover Image: ShutterStock: 1448451

Library of Congress Cataloging-in-Publication Data

North, Charles Mark, 1964-
    Good intentions : nine hot-button issues viewed through the eyes of
faith / Charles M. North, Bob Smietana.
        p. cm.
    Includes bibliographical references.
    ISBN-13: 978-0-8024-3462-3
    ISBN-10: 0-8024-3462-2
    1. Economics—Religious aspects. 2. Capitalism—Religious aspects.
I. Smietana, Bob, 1965- II. Title.

HB72.N667 2008
261.8—dc22

                                                            2007042220

To Rebekah and Emily, Lindsay, and Allie
C.M.N.

For Paul Smietana (1966-2006), who knew that
God cares about doing the little things right.
Peace to his memory.
Bob S.

CONTENTS

1. IS THE ROAD TO ECONOMIC HELL PAVED WITH GOOD INTENTIONS?

On a frozen December day in late 2002, more than seven hundred people stood in line on the vacant lot at 35 Revere Beach Parkway in Medford, Massachusetts, waiting for a taste of heaven—or at least as close to heaven as a deep-fried, sugar-coated, hot-off-the-conveyer-belt doughnut can bring you.

That vacant lot, once the site of a Bickford's pancake house, was the future home of the first Krispy Kreme Doughnut store in Massachusetts, the doughnut capital of the free world. According to *The Wall Street Journal*, there are more than twelve hundred doughnut shops in Boston—or "one for every 5,143 people." (Nearby Providence, Rhode Island, the *Journal* reported, has a doughnut shop for every 4,226 people.) More importantly, New England is also home to Dunkin Donuts, the king of the American doughnut industry, and Krispy Kreme was invading its territory. The groundbreaking for the Medford Krispy Kreme was the first stage of the invasion.

For the occasion, the store owners brought in the Krispy Kreme Mobile Store, a modified eighteen-wheeler equipped with a mini doughnut factory, capable of recreating Krispy Kreme's hallmark: "doughnut theater." Onlookers watched through a glass window as fresh doughnuts were dropped into a lake of boiling shortening, dunked under a waterfall of sugary glaze, then plucked off a conveyer belt and placed in the hands of a hungry customer.

The combination of a secret recipe—purchased in 1933 from Joe LeBeau, a French chef living in New Orleans—and piping-hot delivery made Krispy Kreme irresistible. Originally founded in 1937 by twenty-one-year-old Vernon Rudolph and two friends, it had flourished as a southern chain, only to go through a downturn in the 1970s when the company was bought by Beatrice Foods. Then, in the 1980s, the company was sold to private investors. A new CEO named Scott Livengood revitalized Krispy Kreme, focusing on its nostalgic image and the magic of doughnut theater. The company began growing like gangbusters.

In early 2003, Krispy Kreme had 292 stores with $492 million in sales, earning $33 million in profits for the previous year. By 2004, according to *CFO* magazine, Krispy Kreme "reported $665.6 million in sales and $94.7 million in operating profit from its nearly 400 locations, including stores in Australia, Canada, and South Korea." Company stock, which debuted at $21, soon climbed to nearly $50 a share.

During their first week in business, new stores would sell nearly half a million dollars' worth of doughnuts and coffee, with hundreds of customers camped out as opening day approached. When the Medford store opened on the morning of June 24, 2003, nearly 250 people were already waiting outside. Opening-day sales were $73,813, according to the *Lowell Sun*—a new company record. By week's end, sales had exceeded $500,000.

Two weeks later, on July 7, *Fortune* magazine pronounced Krispy Kreme "the hottest brand in America." In his cover story, reporter Andy Serwer described Krispy Kreme's success in religious terms: The company's annual meeting was "sacred ground";

its employees didn't just make doughnuts—they had "a calling"; and its success was a testament to "the American dream."

"It may seem grimly amusing that in a time of economic pain, corporate scandals, and troubles overseas, this company should be growing so explosively," wrote Serwer. He went on to say:

> But the Krispy Kreme story is about far more than comfort food—the company's wild success in this hard environment is a tale of shrewdness, original thinking, and brinksmanship. The yarn is part Southern gothic—as in long (try six decades) and tortured, replete with heroes and even Yankee villains—and part sophisticated yet homey marketing that helped create the hottest brand in the land.

Serwer ended his article this way: "The world is always filled with unknowns, never more so than right now. With all that's wrong out there, sometimes it's easy to lose focus on the big picture. So take a second and ask yourself: Is the American dream still alive? Is Krispy Kreme for real? Don't bet against it."

Krispy Kreme was on top of the world. It had a product that inspired fanatical devotion, massive brand awareness (despite doing virtually no advertising), soaring profits, and one of the hottest stocks on Wall Street. It even embodied the American dream.

But then the world turned.

Atkins Diet mania hit the United States and carbohydrates became public enemy number one. Sales of Krispy Kreme doughnuts started shrinking. According to *Snack Food & Wholesale Bakery*, a trade publication, Krispy Kreme lost $21.7 million in the first nine months of 2004. By the end of the year, Livengood and six of the company's top executives were fired in an accounting scandal. The company stock fell from nearly $50 to less than $4. Eighty stores closed. In 2005, Krispy Kreme lost

$197 million. In less than a year, Krispy Kreme—as one business magazine put it—had become "fried."

What went wrong? Two things stand out.

First, Krispy Kreme made too many doughnuts. According to *Making Dough*, a chronicle of "The 12 Secret Ingredients to Krispy Kreme's Sweet Success," the company's 292 stores made a whopping two billion of them in 2003. Dunkin Donuts, with more than five thousand stores worldwide—more than seventeen times the stores of Krispy Kreme—made only 2.3 billion doughnuts.

Each Krispy Kreme store could pump out between 48,000 and 120,000 doughnuts a day, but those stores, which cost $2–3 million each, needed nearly twice the sales of a Dunkin Donuts to break even. Even worse for Krispy Kreme, the company made almost a third of its revenue ($152.7 million, reports *CFO* magazine) selling doughnut mix and machinery to franchises. When sales at franchises fell, the company felt a double whammy.

Krispy Kreme was also in the wrong business, at least in New England. Its rivals—Dunkin Donuts and Honey Dew Donuts—made most of their money selling coffee, whereas Krispy Kreme made most of its money on doughnuts; coffee represented only 10 percent of its total business. Even *Fortune*'s Adam Serwer later admitted that Krispy Kreme's doughnuts—no matter how tasty they were—were not enough to draw customers into stores on a regular basis.

"Starbucks you can go to every single day," he said on CNN's *In the Money* after Krispy Kreme's troubles became public. "I happen to go there twice a day. . . . [But if] you go into Krispy Kreme every day, you've got a problem. That's too much."

Too many doughnuts. Not enough coffee. A business plan so flawed that nothing—not heavenly doughnuts, not Southern gothic myths, not America's hottest brand, and not even the American dream—could save Krispy Kreme from disaster.

Everyone involved with Krispy Kreme—the company's leaders,

the media, the investors, and the analysts—fell in love with a magical, wonderful idea. Hot glazed doughnuts produced in a theater. They even talked about it in religious terms. But nobody asked, "Will this work? Who's going to eat all these doughnuts?"

Krispy Kreme's executives thought their ideas were so special—so *blessed*—that the normal economic rules didn't apply to them. They were wrong, of course, and it cost them dearly.

"There's Never Ever Ever Been a Show Like *VeggieTales*"

Phil Vischer had a big idea.

In the early 1990s, Phil Vischer, an aspiring computer animator and Bible-school dropout—he'd been kicked out for failing to attend chapel—began working on an idea for a computer-animated video series for kids. Starring a pair of Abbott and Costello-like singing vegetables that loved Jesus, the series featured Bible stories remixed in a style that was part Monty Python, part *Joseph and the Amazing Technicolor Dreamcoat*.

Vischer provided the voice of Bob the Tomato. His friend, Mike Nawrocki, played Larry the Cucumber. They called the series *VeggieTales*. The company was christened Big Idea Productions. Working on a shoestring budget out of a six hundred-square-foot storefront on Foster Avenue in Chicago, Vischer and several friends labored feverishly on the project for months—at one point working fifty-seven hours straight. Money was so tight that Big Idea couldn't even pay its heating bill. In his book *Me, Myself, and Bob*, Vischer recalls coming into the office late one frigid evening to find his friend Robert Ellis dressed in a parka and covered in a blanket, sitting next to a space heater while hard at work on "Where's God When I'm S-Scared?" the first *VeggieTales* episode.

This first episode was completed a week before Christmas 1993, just in time to ship out the five hundred preordered copies. It wasn't enough copies to pay for production costs, but Vischer remained hopeful. Within a year, *VeggieTales* began to catch on, thanks in large part to college students who worked at local Christian bookstores. They became big fans and played the video over and over again. The parents shopping in the stores saw "Where's God When I'm S-Scared?" and started buying it in droves.

In 1994, Big Idea sold fifty thousand copies. By 1997, they'd sold more than two million videos and had moved to a new office in Chicago. Big Idea had $4 million in the bank and no debt. "For the first time in our four year history, making payroll was no longer a concern," Vischer wrote in *Me, Myself, and Bob*. "Money was coming in faster than we could spend it."

Dick Leach, owner of Lyrick Studios (the creators of *Barney*), got ahold of a *VeggieTales* video and signed on as Big Idea's distributor. By 1999, annual sales reached seven million videos— bringing in close to $40 million in revenue. In an interview with *Christianity Today*, Vischer called it a "hockey stick" growth curve: straight up with no end in sight.

Big Idea was featured in *The Wall Street Journal* and *Time* magazine, and it even appeared on *The Today Show*. Wal-Mart began selling the videos in massive quantities. And Hollywood was knocking on Vischer's door. His big idea had become a reality. So he came up with a bigger one.

Inspired by a desire to tell as many kids as possible that God loved them—and having read *Built to Last*, the best-selling business book by Jim Collins—Vischer came up with a "Big, Hairy, Audacious Goal": to build Big Idea from an animation studio producing a single video series into a media giant capable of challenging Nickelodeon and the Cartoon Network. Big Idea would become the new Disney, Vischer thought. God had blessed his first dream, and he was sure that God would bless this new one as well.

Unfortunately, Vischer, a goateed, bespectacled, natural-born storyteller, was not an empire builder—not really a CEO. And unlike Walt Disney, whose brother Roy was the brains behind the company, Vischer never found a business partner who could bring his vision to life. Instead, armed with a history of ever-rising sales, Big Idea built a master plan on shaky ground. It projected that sales would grow from $40 million in 1999 to $125 million in 2002. The company expanded, hiring staff and borrowing and spending money as if it were a Hollywood studio instead of a company that made half-hour, direct-to-video shows for kids. Vischer would later admit that he took his eyes off the money, believing that his dream was enough.

But instead of growing, sales went flat in 2000. Suddenly, Big Idea could no longer afford to pay its bills. To survive, drastic cuts were needed. That meant laying off staff, whom Vischer had come to see as family. Layoffs, he believed, could not possibly be God's will. Like many entrepreneurs, Vischer became so closely attached to his business that he couldn't let go. Committed to saving the company and the jobs of the people he loved, he risked everything to keep Big Idea alive.

Big Idea needed a miracle. The company's last hope was *Jonah: A VeggieTales Movie*, its first feature film. Made for around $10 million dollars, the movie could have saved Big Idea had it been an unexpected hit on the order of *My Big Fat Greek Wedding*. On opening night, as the first box office results came in, there was a glimmer of hope. Reports from the first showings were higher than expected. But box office receipts began to slip as the night wore on, and before the end of the evening, it was clear that there would be no miracle. The next morning, Vischer announced that most of Big Idea's animators would be laid off.

Not long afterward, Lyrick Studios sued Big Idea for breach of contract (in 2001, following the death of Lyrick president Dick Leach, Big Idea had switched distributors, signing with Warner Home Video). In April 2003, a Dallas jury ruled in Lyrick's favor, awarding it $11 million in damages. The suit was eventually thrown out on appeal, but that was too late to save Vischer and Big Idea.

Big Idea went bankrupt and was sold to Classic Media for enough money to pay off its debtors. The company survives and still makes *VeggieTales* videos with a small creative staff led by Mike Nawrocki, the voice of Larry the Cucumber, but the vision of becoming the next Disney is long gone. A big idea was not enough.

Results Matter

Results matter—whether you are making heavenly doughnuts or creating computer-animated vegetables that love Jesus. And more often than not, they are predictable. That, in a nutshell, is the point of this book. And it might just be one of the most important lessons that *VeggieTales* and Krispy Kreme doughnuts have to teach.

Why aren't good intentions enough? Because we live in a world of scarcity, a world where we can't get everything we want for free. That's one of the first principles that beginning economics students learn. When most people hear the word "economics," they think of stock markets, the Federal Reserve, unemployment reports, and other topics covered in *The Wall Street Journal* or the business section of the local newspaper. But at its core, economics is really about people, about understanding the choices people make when there's not enough to go around.

Economics offers a set of tools to help people make good decisions about how to distribute limited resources in the most effective way possible, to help people understand the consequences of the decisions that they make, and to help people understand how others will likely react to those decisions.

Economists don't try to make us feel good about ourselves when we shouldn't. Nor do they try to prop up bad decisions that were sentimentally made. Rather, economics is about helping people make their lives better by using information to make effective choices.

In the chapters that follow, we'll look at some of the most pressing issues confronting Christians in the twenty-first century. Issues such as poverty and global warming, education and immigration. Issues where the stakes are high, and where the decisions of Christians—how they vote and how they spend their money— have real-world consequences for millions of people.

We'll look at good intentions, to be sure, but we'll ask another important question as well: Does it work?

A case in point . . .

The ABCs of HIV

In the late 1980s, the African country of Uganda faced a life-or-death crisis. Fifteen percent of the population was infected with HIV (the virus that causes AIDS), one of the highest rates in the world. Millions of people had the disease. Unless the epidemic was contained, millions more would get it, and the country risked falling into ruin.

With little money and an overtaxed health-care system—as Harvard AIDS researcher Ted Green put it, "even something as simple as aspirin was in short supply"—Uganda's situation seemed desperate. But then something remarkable happened. The prevalence of AIDS—the number of people infected with HIV—began to drop dramatically, down to about 6 percent of the population. While still a serious threat, the epidemic was contained. Uganda remains the only African country to have reduced its AIDS prevalence. The country's efforts in AIDS prevention seemed nothing short of miraculous.

The key to Uganda's success was a program called ABC—an acronym for "Abstain," "Be Faithful," and "Use a Condom." It worked this way: Teenagers were asked to delay having sex until they were married, or at least until they were older; those in sexual relationships were told not to look for sex in other places; and those at high risk of contracting AIDS, mainly soldiers and long-distance truckers, were given condoms and told to use them. Fighting AIDS became a "patriotic duty" for Ugandans. The government mobilized all sectors of Ugandan society—government, education, religion, entertainment—to urge citizens to change their sexual practices. One of the main focuses was promoting fidelity in monogamous relationships, otherwise known as "Zero Grazing." The idea was to make sure that everyone knew "that AIDS was a threat," Green says. "You will die if you get it, so you must change your behavior." The total cost of the program was just over $21 million dollars.

Two well-financed movements have waged a culture-war battle over the Ugandan turnaround, mainly on ideological grounds. One side is made up of conservative Christian activists who favor the A-approach of promoting abstinence. The other side is comprised of AIDS activists who favor the C-approach of condoms and sex education.

The organization Human Rights Watch, a C-proponent, has accused United States government-funded abstinence programs of "hijacking" Uganda's AIDS prevention program. In 2005, the group released a study condemning abstinence programs as putting "Uganda's children at risk of HIV." The study's author, a researcher named Jonathan Cohen, wrote that "abstinence-only programs are a triumph of ideology over public health. Americans should demand that HIV-prevention programs worldwide stick to science."

Meanwhile, after Congress approved President Bush's global AIDS initiative, including funding for abstinence-only programs, groups favoring the A-approach cheered. For example, in a story on Focus on the Family's CitizenLink news service, Thomas Minnery, Focus's vice president of public policy, called the ABC plan a "landmark effort" to ensure that "the only successful approach—abstinence—will be a priority. AIDS sufferers in Africa will no longer continue to be offered only condoms—the same faulty approach that has increased sexually transmitted diseases in America."

When it comes to AIDS prevention, both the A- and C-proponents have good intentions. Both groups want to prevent the suffering of AIDS victims and to spare as many people as possible from the ravages of the disease. Unfortunately, both groups are also wrong.

According to studies by epidemiologists Rand Stoneburner and Daniel Low-Beer, formerly of the World Health Organization, neither abstinence nor condoms were most responsible for the Ugandan miracle. One of their studies, published in a 2004 issue of *Science*, indicates that the "Be faithful" focus of ABC was ultimately the most important component.

Helen Epstein, a biologist and former AIDS field-worker now at Princeton University, called this finding "The Fidelity Fix." Reporting in *The New York Times Magazine*, Epstein wrote that "as experts come to understand more about the African AIDS epidemic, it seems clear that regular sexual contact with more than one person is the key human behavior that enables the rapid spread of H.I.V."

It turns out that the spread of AIDS in sub-Saharan Africa is exacerbated by what Epstein called "concurrence"—long-term sexual relationships with more than one person, which are common in the region. Concurrence, says Epstein, "links sexually active people up in a giant network, not only to one another but also to the partners of their partner's partners—and to the partners of those partners, and so on—via a web of sexual relationships that can extend across huge regions." When one person in the web gets HIV, he or she can quickly infect the whole web. Promoting fidelity in monogamous relationships through "Be Faithful" or "Zero Grazing" approaches can cut those webs and hamper the disease's ability to spread.

Unfortunately, with secular AIDS groups and conservatives locked in a culture-war death match over "abstinence versus condoms," no one appears to be paying attention to this information. In a piece called "God and the Fight Against AIDS," Epstein reports that the "Zero Grazing" strategy has been largely abandoned in Uganda—a development she refers to as "a great shame."

Christian Principles

Two caveats as we proceed.

The first is that we are not theologians. The authors of this book are an economist and a religion journalist. We are not attempting to tell Christians what decisions to make, and we offer no magic formulas. Instead, we will combine some basic Christian principles with the tools of economics to look at some pressing social issues and ask, "How can we apply these Christian principles in an effective way? How can our actions produce outcomes that match our values?"

One such guiding principle comes from the book *Kingdom Ethics* by Christian ethicists Glen Stassen and David Gushee. "All material goods," these authors write, "including the most basic—food—must be viewed as God's good gifts, divine provision for all humankind." The goal of Christian economics is to get God's gifts into the hands of as many of God's people as possible. This is easier said than done, but the Bible establishes it as a guiding principle.

A few additional guiding principles taken from the Scriptures:

- Everyone deserves a fair shake.

- Everyone works.

- God wants people to prosper—to be able to make a living.

- Some people, for a number of reasons, will fall behind and lose the means to make a living.

■ God wants those people to be restored, so they have access to the means of making a living.

The second caveat is that economics is not an exact science. After asking "Will it work?" economists often ask a second question: "What comes next?" Economic solutions often produce unintended results—results that will then require new solutions of their own.

No Jobs, No Babies

For most of the latter half of the twentieth century, Europe seemed like a paradise for workers. Employees in most Western European countries enjoyed long vacations (at least six weeks a year), shorter working hours, guaranteed pensions, and—best of all—nearly unlimited job security. Most countries passed "employment protection" laws, aimed at giving workers long-term, stable employment. These rules required high levels of benefits and made firing workers more difficult and expensive. In effect, most people had jobs for life. Or more precisely, most *men* had jobs for life.

Unfortunately, while the rules benefited prime-age, native-born males who already had jobs, they made it difficult for new workers to find jobs. Many women, younger workers, and immigrants could not locate work because most European positions were already filled. Over time, job-security laws led to high unemployment rates—the first of their unintended consequences.

Another consequence was that many European women stopped having babies. In the United States, the total fertility rate is 2.09, or roughly at the replacement rate. But in the European Union, the rate is 1.47 children per woman, a rate so low that the European Union's population is expected to decline over the next fifty years. The most noticeable declines are expected in the Western European nations of Germany, Italy, Portugal, and Spain; in the formerly communist nations of Bulgaria, the Czech Republic, Hungary, Poland, Romania, Slovakia, Latvia, Lithuania, and Estonia; and in Greece (see table 1.1).

Alicia Adsera, an economist and demographer at Princeton University, has an explanation for this phenomenon. She argues that women have fewer babies in countries where labor markets create uncertainty over future employment. One might think that high unemployment—and lots of free time—would lead to more babies, but this isn't so in Europe. Adsera's research shows that European women have had fewer babies in countries where unemployment rates are high and part-time work is hard to find. These countries often have fewer women in the workforce as well. Adsera believes that unemployment and a lack of part-time work reduce long-term income to the point that some women choose to delay having children.

What does employment protection have to do with fertility? A lot, given Adsera's research findings. Employment-protection laws helped to create high unemployment and a lack of part-time jobs—the things associated with reduced fertility; they had a long-term effect of creating more uncertainty for the next generation of young workers, especially women. And that generation responded by having fewer kids.

Why does this matter? The shrinking population of young people means either that individuals will have to work deeper into old age or that less of the population will be contributing to economic production. Similarly, with fewer young people to generate income (and taxes), there are serious concerns about the future viability of social insurance programs that support the elderly, as well as of national health care programs. In short, the European social welfare state—indeed, European well-being—depends on the continued presence of young workers who are simply not being born.

In the aftermath of World War II, European policymakers

TABLE 1.1	TOTAL FERTILITY RATES, SELECTED NATIONS
COUNTRY	**TOTAL FERTILITY RATE** (Children/Born Woman)
Austria	1.36
Belgium	1.64
Bulgaria	1.38
Czech Republic	1.21
Denmark	1.74
Finland	1.73
France	1.84
Germany	1.39
Greece	1.34
Ireland	1.86
Italy	1.28
Netherlands	1.66
Norway	1.78
Poland	1.25
Portugal	1.47
Romania	1.37
Russia	1.28
Slovakia	1.33
Spain	1.28
Sweden	1.66
United Kingdom	1.66
TOTAL EUROPEAN UNION	1.47
Canada	1.61
United States	2.09
ENTIRE WORLD	2.59

wanted to provide stable jobs for family breadwinners so that families could thrive, and at first that is what they got. But then a new generation came along and couldn't find jobs. So they ended up unemployed; they delayed marriage; and they had fewer children. And now the very system intended to protect and nurture European families threatens the future success of new families throughout Europe.

Good intentions do not assure good results, and they can at times lead to policies with perverse unintended consequences. As in the rest of life, the road to economic hell is often paved with the best of intentions.

In his book *The Screwtape Letters*, C. S. Lewis's imaginary senior devil gives his nephew advice on how to confuse human beings and lead them into making poor choices.

"The Enemy loves platitudes," Screwtape writes. "Of a proposed course of action He wants men, so far as I can see, to ask very simple questions; is it righteous? is it prudent? is it possible? Now if we can keep men asking 'Is it in accordance with the general movement of our time? Is it progressive or reactionary? Is this the way that History is going?' they will neglect the relevant questions."

Ignoring such "relevant questions" can lead to disaster. In the upcoming chapters, we'll look at some hot-button issues, those whose answers aren't always clear but whose stakes are uniformly high. In each case, we've asked, "What works?" The answers may surprise you—they certainly surprised us—and they may even "feel" wrong at times.

Too often, Christians ask only one question when choosing a course of action—"Is it righteous?"—and forget to ask whether a thing is likewise prudent or possible. But there's nothing righteous about bad decisions. In the case of AIDS prevention, abstinence activists and condom promoters both think that their respective choices are righteous—all involved believe that *they* are doing the right thing. But as Helen Epstein points out, neither side asks if its approach is prudent or possible. As a result, both fail to address the major cause of the AIDS pandemic in sub-Saharan Africa.

The politicians who passed job-protection laws in Europe thought they were doing the right thing as well, but their decisions have led to some very serious consequences—consequences that might be reversed by relaxing a few of the protections at issue or that could demand a different approach altogether.

Whatever the case, one thing is clear: When things do go wrong, and unintended consequences or disastrous results crop up, better to abandon your current path—no matter how noble your reasons for taking it—than continue going the wrong way.

2. IS GREED EVER GOOD?

"For the love of money is the root of all evil."

—PAUL OF TARSUS, 1 TIMOTHY 6:10 (KJV)

"Greed is good."

—GORDON GEKKO, *WALL STREET*

Greed is good.

At least that's what economist Walter Williams thinks every time he goes out to dinner or drives his car. Neither thing would be possible, he believes, if cattle ranchers or autoworkers weren't at least a little bit greedy.

If they were motivated by goodwill instead of greed, those ranchers and autoworkers would be more likely to stay in bed on cold winter mornings—or on most days—rather than going out to work. And Williams would be hungry and walking.

That's what he argues in an essay titled "The Virtue of Greed" for *Capitalism* magazine. "Is there anyone who believes that the reason we have cars is because Detroit assembly-line workers care about us?" he writes. "It's also wonderful that Texas cattle ranchers make the sacrifices of time and effort caring for steer so that New Yorkers can enjoy a steak now and then. Again, is there anyone who believes that ranchers who make these sacrifices do so out of a concern for and feeling the pain of New Yorkers?"

Williams's point is this: When it comes to getting things done, there's nothing quite like greed. "The true reason why we enjoy cars, steaks, and millions of other goods and services is because people care mostly about themselves," he argues.

Williams's praise for greed doesn't stop there. In his essay "Greed Versus Compassion," he says that greed is "the noblest of human motivations"—more powerful than love, compassion, or charity. Love, compassion, and charity might feel better, he says, but greed gets more done.

In his defense, Williams does put some limits on his definition of "greed." For example, he rules out "theft, fraud, tricks, or misrepresentation." Instead, he defines greed as "people being only or mostly concerned with getting the most they can for themselves and not necessarily concerned about the welfare of others."

Williams admits that he uses the word "greed" because it gets people's attention. Most economists talk about "self-interest." But economists agree with Williams on this: People motivated by their own self-interest can accomplish great things.

The Butcher, the Brewer, or the Baker

Williams's belief in the power of self-interest is nothing new. From the start, modern economics has been based on the power of self-interest. For example, in *The Wealth of Nations*, first published in 1776, Adam Smith wrote, "It is not from the benevolence of the butcher, the brewer or the baker that we expect our dinner, but from their regard to their own interests."

This famous quote has come under fire. Critics say that Smith wanted people to be selfish—to be concerned only for themselves. Such a life would obviously violate Christian teaching. University of Leeds economist Douglas Puffert summarizes another critical view as focusing on how economics "is inescapably intertwined with a faulty understanding of human nature and destiny." Because of this, he writes, some Christian critics believe that economic thinking encourages a self-centered, morals-free view of the human person "at the expense of community, love, and human fulfillment."

These critics misinterpret what Adam Smith—and modern economics—are about. Another book by Smith, *The Theory of Moral Sentiments*, talked a lot about self-interest. In particular, it stated that moral rules constrain self-interest. These moral rules exist because people disapprove of one person unfairly hurting another. Without such moral rules, Smith said, human society "would crumble into nothing."

When Adam Smith talked about self-interest—and even when Walter Williams talks about "greed"—he meant a *constrained* self-interest, a desire to be better off without unfairly hurting anyone else. He was not talking about a valueless, unrestrained greed.

This is clear from seeing what else Smith said in *Wealth of Nations* regarding the butcher, brewer, and baker. The baker sells you bread because it profits him. In the same way, *you* benefit from buying the bread, because you can get a good quality loaf at a price below the cost of baking it yourself. And by paying for it, you got that bread much more reliably than you could by simply begging it from the baker the way a dog begs for table scraps.

Smith's logic may be easier to see if we reverse this scenario. If Smith were advising the baker rather than the customers, he would still tell the baker to appeal to the buyer's self-interest. "Don't ask your customer to buy your bread because you really need money to buy new shoes for the children, or to pay the rent. Appeal to the customer's self-interest by baking good bread at a fair price, and you shall have the money you need."

Self-interest has an incredible power to organize the production and distribution of the various goods and services we use. Rather than organizing from the top down, economies function better from the bottom up, with each person pursuing their own self-interest. A person works hard to make something others value, wrote Smith in *Wealth of Nations*. In doing so, "he intends only his own gain, and he is in this, as in many other cases, led by an invisible hand to promote an end which was no part of his intention."

This "invisible hand" creates order and mutual benefit out of the self-interested actions of each member of society. The invisible hand may be a mere metaphor for the organizing power of self-interest when put to use in a well-functioning market, but that power is real enough. Self-interest can take the actions of tens of thousands of people and integrate them into a thriving, functioning society. That's what the owners of Linden Labs discovered not long ago.

Second Life

Linden Labs runs an online game called *Second Life*—a virtual world in which tens of thousands of players can interact at the same time. Journalist Annalee Newitz covered the game for *Popular Science* magazine. Describing her first visit to *Second Life*, she writes:

> I'm standing in an airy train station surrounded by rolling, wooded hills. Distant sounds of birds and trickling water reach my ears over a low buzz of chitchat from the people around me. They have come from all over North America to meet here, and now they're lounging on couches and standing in sociable little clots. Ballerinas are talking to men in body armor, while guys in suits show off their dance moves to aliens and ladies with wings. I try not to stare.
>
> Or rather, a digital version of me called an avatar tries not to stare. I'm sitting at my computer, and my point of view hovers about three feet behind as I use the arrow buttons on my keyboard to amble toward the street outside. Next to me, a blue elf and a towering woman in a black cape tap on invisible keyboards

that hover in the air. I can hear the click of the keys, and cartoon speech bubbles near their heads reveal that they're discussing computer programming.

The problem that Linden Labs faced when starting *Second Life* was this: How do you create a virtual world that mimics the vitality and diversity of the real world? The easy part was creating the geography of *Second Life*—cities and towns, oceans and islands. The hard part? Bringing that virtual world to life.

Paying programmers to create all the inhabitants of *Second Life*—known as avatars—and all the clothes, houses, vehicles, stores, and other accessories needed to bring the world to life would cost hundreds of millions of dollars. Then Linden Labs discovered the wonder-working power of self-interest. Rather than create everything at the company's San Francisco headquarters—like most online gaming companies do—Linden Labs asked players to help create the world of *Second Life*. Not only that, but it gave players the chance to make money doing so.

The company's programmers did the initial organizing for *Second Life*; they wrote the software that players would use and included simple tools so that players could build everything they needed—from bodies and clothes to buildings and boutiques; and now they merely maintain the massive servers that keep the virtual world spinning along.

But the real breakthrough for *Second Life* came in 2003, when Linden Labs decided to allow players to keep the rights to anything they made. To give players even more incentive to create, the company created a stable currency—the Linden dollar—so players can sell their creations to other players. (Players can trade one U.S. dollar for about three hundred Linden dollars.)

The result was a flourishing world filled with mermaids and motorcycles, winged creatures and weddings, where avatars shaped liked human beings mingle in shops with those that look like they just stepped off the set of the latest *Star Wars* movie. It's a place where "real world" companies like American Express set up shop. *Second Life* has garnered so much attention that the Reuters news service recently opened a news bureau there to report on this virtual world.

By the winter of 2006, more than two million people had signed up to use the game, with more than twenty thousand logged on at any given moment. The combined gross domestic product of *Second Life* was $64 million dollars, according to *Popular Science*. And according to *Business Week*, at least three thousand *Second Life* entrepreneurs make $20,000 or more a year.

The secret of *Second Life*'s success? According to Robert D. Hof, who authored the *Business Week* story, the company tapped into the creativity and resourcefulness of its players.

"After all my travels around *Second Life*, it's becoming apparent that virtual worlds, most of all this one, tap into something very powerful: the talent and hard work of everyone inside," he writes. "Residents spend a quarter of the time they're logged in, a total of nearly 23,000 hours a day, creating things that become part of the world, available to everyone else."

When Hof asked officials at Linden Labs how many programmers it would take to duplicate the efforts of players, they told him it would take a team of more than four thousand—and cost more than four hundred million dollars. The players of *Second Life*, working on their own, organized the job for much less. Because of the enjoyment and novelty of playing the game, they likely had a good time in the process.

Recycling the Victorian Way

The invisible hand of self-interest can work as well in real life as it does in the virtual world of *Second Life*. In *The Ghost Map*, a book about the 1854 London cholera outbreak, Steven Johnson provides another example of the organizing power of self-interest.

At that time, London's population had skyrocketed to more

than two million people. Unfortunately, the city's infrastructure—in particular, trash collection and sewage—was virtually nonexistent.

Then something remarkable happened. Without any central planning or direction from London's leaders, the city's underclass created a grassroots recycling army. Johnson begins his book with a list of them: "bone pickers, rag gatherers, pure-finders, dredgermen, mud-larks, sewer-hunters, dustmen, night soil men, bunters, toshers, shoremen."

Each of the recyclers sold their salvage off to a section of London's thriving economy. Johnson describes how night soil men sold human waste to the farmers outside the city to use as fertilizer. Pure-finders sold pure (dog feces) to tanners, who used it to remove the lime from their leather. Bone pickers sold their findings to bone boilers, while toshers sold off the copper they recovered from the muck of the Thames River.

Life was difficult for these recyclers. As Johnson puts it, they "lived in a world of excrement and death." But the author also pays homage to the recyclers and considers them heroes. He writes:

> We're naturally inclined to consider these scavengers tragic figures, and to fulminate against a system that allowed so many thousands to eke out a living foraging through human waste. . . . But such social outrage should be accompanied by a measure of wonder and respect: without any central planning coordinating their actions, without any education at all, this itinerant underclass managed to conjure up a system for processing and sorting the waste generated by two million people.

Again, none of the toshers or night soil men toiled for the public good. Instead, each acted out of self-interest. Each was trying to save their own skin, feed their own family. But together, these recyclers created a thing of wonders.

Gordon Gekko: "Greed Is Good"

Adam Smith called this process of creating order out of seeming chaos the "invisible hand." Gordon Gekko—Michael Douglas's character in the Oliver Stone film *Wall Street*—puts it more simply: "Greed is good."

Near the middle of the film, Gekko addresses the shareholders of the fictional Teldar Paper Company. Gekko, a ruthless corporate raider, wants the shareholders to sell the company off in a hostile takeover that will mostly benefit himself, being the company's biggest shareholder. (The speech was inspired by a similar one given in 1986 by the notorious insider trader Ivan Boesky.)

Gekko begins by attacking the company's management:

Teldar Paper has 33 different vice presidents, each earning over 200 thousand dollars a year. Now, I have spent the last two months analyzing what all these guys do, and I still can't figure it out. One thing I do know is that our paper company lost 110 million dollars last year, and I'll bet that half of that was spent in all the paperwork going back and forth between all these vice presidents.

The new law of evolution in corporate America seems to be survival of the unfittest. Well, in my book you either do it right or you get eliminated.

In the last seven deals that I've been involved with, there were 2.5 million stockholders who have made a pretax profit of twelve billion dollars. . . . I am not a destroyer of companies. I am a liberator of them!

Then Gekko goes for the kill.

"The point is, ladies and gentlemen, that greed—for lack of a better word—is good," he says.

Greed is right. Greed works. Greed clarifies, cuts through, and captures the essence of the evolutionary spirit. Greed, in all of its forms—greed for life, for money, for love, knowledge—has marked the upward surge of mankind. And greed—you mark my words—will not only save Teldar Paper, but that other malfunctioning corporation called the USA.

Not So Fast

All this talk about greed being good is unsettling for Christians. Jesus, after all, was no fan of self-interest. Quite the opposite, as Mark 8:34–36 attests:

Then he called the crowd to him along with his disciples and said: "If anyone would come after me, he must deny himself and take up his cross and follow me. For whoever wants to save his life will lose it, but whoever loses his life for me and for the gospel will save it. What good is it for a man to gain the whole world, yet forfeit his soul?"

The apostle Paul echoes these words in the book of Philippians: "Do nothing out of selfish ambition or vain conceit, but in humility consider others better than yourselves. Each of you should look not only to your own interests, but also to the interests of others" (Philippians 2:3–4). Then he adds in 1 Timothy 6:10 "The love of money is a root of all kinds of evil."

Since the time of Jesus and Paul, Christians have been suspicious of greed. Christian practice and ethics embrace self-denial and putting the needs of other people first. "Looking out for number one" means risking spiritual peril. As Jesus put it, what good is it to gain the whole world and lose your soul in the process? Even when it's cast in the mildest terms—as "thrift" or "industriousness"—Christians are still wary of greed.

The early church fathers considered greed one of the seven

deadly sins. Phyllis Tickle, in her book *Greed* (part of an Oxford University Press series on the seven deadly sins), recounts one of the classic Christian portrayals of Greed, found in the *Psychomachia*—or "Battle for the Soul"— by Aurelius Clemens Prudentius. Prudentius, who lived around 405 CE, depicted each of the seven deadly sins—Pride, Greed, Lust, Envy, Gluttony, Anger, and Sloth—as human characters. Greed is a scavenger who searches the field of battle after Lust has been driven off. As Tickle describes her, Greed is accompanied by a host of henchmen—Care, Hunger, Fear, Anxiety, Perjury, Dread, Fraud, Fabrication, Sleeplessness, and Sordidness—who roam the field "like ravenous wolves."

Once defeated, Greed undergoes a transformation. "Laying her weapons down, she changes robes and her demeanor to ones of simple austerity," says Tickle. Greed the sin becomes Thrift, a virtue. But the transformation is a trap and ensnares Greed's victims. Soon, says Prudentius, "the wicked fiend finds them cheerful victims happy to live in her shackles."

Tickle sums things up this way:

> The *Psychomachia* is the story that established at a popular level Greed's sex, her image as a mother of a deadly clan, her worrisome ability to change into false virtue upon demand, and more suggested than stated, the understanding that greed is actually the sin of apostasy, of desiring a life subject to human control over a life of vulnerable trust in the unseen.

Tickle also offers a glimpse of Prudentius's original Latin: "*Quod tantis cladibus, aeuum/mundane invuoluat populi damestque gehennae.*" Or in English, "Greed wraps the lives of men in calamities that they only escape when they are thrown into hell's fires."

So What's the Difference?

What's a Christian to do with all this? Is there really a difference between "greed" and "self-interest"? Is greed a vice or a virtue in disguise? Does the pursuit of Adam Smith's "self-interest" put a Christian's soul in jeopardy?

Laura Nash has thought a lot about the conflict between self-interest and faith. The managing partner of a hedge fund, she's also a former senior lecturer at the Harvard School of Business, former faculty member at Harvard Divinity School, and author of several books on faith and work.

In November 2005, she spoke to Christian business executives at St. Paul's Cathedral in London during a conference on "Finding Personal Wholeness in the Changing World of Work." The conference's brochure was telling. It asked, "What can the Christian faith do to prevent work from becoming a destructive monster?"

In her speech, she asked, "At what point and in what proportion do I attend to my own interests after attending to those of others?"

Her answer was surprising. Act out of faith, not fear. This involves healing the soul-sickness of which Prudentius warned. Nash also said that solving the conflict between self-interest and faith requires imagination—the ability to see how to create a path between the way things are and the way things could be.

One step toward resolving the conflict between self-interest and faith is to admit that Gordon Gekko is partially right. Greed is a sin, but self-interest can be good. Self-interest can create.

In interviewing businesspeople for her book *Church on Sunday, Work on Monday*, Nash discovered a chasm between how businesspeople and their pastors saw economics. Pastors and church leaders talked in restrictive terms about the need to limit greed. The businesspeople in their congregations had a different view.

"Business people took a positive, additive view: faith was about expanding economic opportunity for more people through business success," says Nash. "For the business person, business was about solving problems and creating prosperity, and it centered on specific activities."

Greedy Hippos

A second step toward reconciling self-interest and faith is to recognize destructive potential of self-interest—how easily it can lead to greed. Self-interest, it turns out, is a lot like Pablo Escobar's hippos.

In the early 1980s, at the height of his power, Colombian drug lord Pablo Escobar, who in 1989 was named by *Forbes* magazine as one of the seven wealthiest people on earth, built Hacienda Napoles, a five thousand five hundred-acre estate complete with a bullring, an airstrip, a mock-Jurassic Park with concrete dinosaurs, and a wild animal park with hundreds of wild animals—including camels, giraffes, ostriches, and elephants. Then there were the four hippos, each weighing close to three thousand pounds, that roamed the twelve man-made lakes on the estate.

When Escobar was finally killed in 1994, the Colombian government moved to take possession of Hacienda Napoles and realized that they had a six-ton problem on their hands: What to do with the hippos? There was no easy solution.

Hippos, despite their tubby appearance and stubby legs, are deadly. Deadlier, it turns out, than great white sharks, lions, cobras, alligators, or grizzly bears, at least when it comes to people. Hippos kill more people each year than any other animal in the world, according to *The Times* of London. Unsuspecting tourists who get too close to an angry hippo may find themselves being stomped to death by something like a three thousand-pound bolt of lightning.

While the other animals on Escobar's former estate were donated to zoos or sold—or died off—the hippos remained. Faced with the daunting choice of moving the hippos or setting up an elaborate system to feed and sustain them (hippos eat one hundred pounds of grass a day and can't be contained by barbed wire or other fences), Colombian officials decided to let nature take care of the hippos. Besides, the government was locked in a long and expensive battle with Escobar's widow for control of the estate. While the government fought with Mrs. Escobar in court, refugees from Colombia's war on drugs settled on the estate and raised cattle there. In the meantime, the Colombian government hoped the hippos would eventually starve to death. But the hippos had other ideas.

As the *Los Angeles Times* reported recently, the hippos, motivated by self-interest without any constraints, solved a complicated problem—how to survive in a foreign land halfway around the world from their homes. They had a few advantages, one of which was that there were no natural predators for hippos in South America. Also, hippos have fairly simple needs, as James Doherty, the general curator at the Bronx Zoo, told *The New York Times* in 2003. "If it's green, they'll eat it, and they need water, lots of water, and they need space," he said.

Left to their own devices, the hippos learned to "forage like cows." Before long, the original four had multiplied into sixteen and began expanding their territory. They wandered off the estate and started exploring nearby rivers—sometimes smashing through fences to get there. Not much, it turns out, can stand in the way of a motivated hippo.

Their self-interest—what Walter Williams labels "greed"— got out of control. And before long, a six-ton problem had become a twenty-four-ton problem with no solution in sight.

Oliver Stone's *Wall Street* gives another example of the destructive power of greed without boundaries. The film ends with the downfall of Gordon Gekko, who is indicted for insider trading. And what brought him to his knees? Gekko lied.

He left out one small but vital detail in his "greed is good" speech. Gekko made most of his money on insider trading—the same crime that brought down stockbrokers Ivan Boesky and Michael Milkin in the 1980s and, more recently, landed Martha Stewart in jail. It turns out that the creative power of self-interest can't work without trust and ethical boundaries.

The creators—and players—of *Second Life* found this out the hard way in the fall of 2006, when their new world almost crashed, all because of a little program called CopyBot. The program, created by a group of *Second Life* players, allowed users to copy anything in the game. Rather than pay for items, CopyBot allowed players to—in effect—steal them. The program caused a near panic until Linden Labs made using Copybot a "term of service" violation, effectively banning the program from the game. At least for a little while, *Second Life's* thriving but fragile economy was safe.

A Fine Line

As we've already seen, the idea that trust and self-interest are intertwined dates all the way back to Adam Smith's view that self-interest must be constrained by morality, or else society crumbles. That's what happens to Gordon Gekko's world in *Wall Street*: without constraint, greed consumes him.

A constrained self-interest consistent with The Golden Rule—"Do unto others as you would have them do unto you"—should be sufficient as a basis for an economic system. But it still leaves the questions many theologians ask: "Can a system built on self-interest truly be good? Wouldn't a system be better if it were built on valuing the well-being of the whole community—especially the least of these?"

When he wrote *Wealth of Nations*, Smith faced a dilemma. On the one hand, in Smith's time, as in our time, human beings were increasingly dependent on one another for the basics of life. Even then, it didn't make sense for people to do everything for themselves: grow their own food, make their own clothes, build their own homes, chop their own firewood, make their own tools or paper, and create the countless other items that civilized people need. On the other hand, people only had so many close ties with other people; they could not form friendships with every person who could create what they needed in life.

The nature of modern commerce is that we trade with untold thousands of people we never meet. There is simply no way that we could befriend each and every one of them and thereby obtain through their kindness and benevolence all of the things we want. We can't rely on the good intentions of others to make sure we have food to eat, clothes to wear, and roofs over our heads.

In a world of specialization, a system based on benevolence won't work. Instead, self-interest—the constrained variety of greed that Walter Williams talks about—seems to be the next best thing.

So no, greed, as theologians describe it, is not good. But in the real world of daily life, the line between Adam Smith's "self-interest" and Gordon Gekko's "greed" is likely to be a fine (and blurry) one. If we zealously stamp out greed, we may do more harm than good.

That's the lesson that the trustees of Harvard University learned recently.

A few years ago, word got out that some of the top staff at Harvard Management Company, which manages Harvard University's $29 billion endowment, had received $78.4 million in bonuses in 2004; and in 2005, they received $56.8 million, according to *The Boston Globe*. The size of the bonuses, along with the size of staff salaries, ticked off a group of alumni, who led a protest campaign to reduce the compensation. With the best of intentions, protest leader William Strauss told *The New York*

Times that it was "unseemly for Harvard employees to make that kind of money." "This is a nonprofit university," he told *Times* columnist Joseph Nocera. "It's just inappropriate."

Because of the protest, Jack R. Meyer, head of Harvard Management, left his post, taking several of his top fund managers with him. In 2006, the new managers earned $13.3 million in salary and bonuses. In the eyes of many in Harvard Yard, greed was conquered and all was put right.

There was just one problem. Under Meyer's leadership, the Harvard endowment posted higher results than virtually every other endowment in the United States The only fund manager to outperform Meyer, according to the *Times*, was David Swenson of Yale.

In the year that Meyer left, the Harvard Endowment earned a return of 16.7 percent, "about average for big university endowments," the *Globe* reported. Unfortunately, that was "far below the cream of the crop, which gained twenty percent or more"—a difference that was worth, at least at Harvard, more than $600 million.

THE POOR YOU WILL
ALWAYS HAVE WITH YOU

"This statement, made by Jesus in Matthew 26:11, remains one of His most famous—and misunderstood—comments. More often than you would think, Christians quote this passage as an excuse for inaction. In essence, they ask, "What's the point of trying to pull people out of poverty if the poor will always be with us?"

But opening the Bible and looking at the verse in context leads to a different conclusion. Recall the setting in Matthew 26: Two days before the Last Supper, a woman in Bethany anointed Jesus with very expensive perfume. This angered some of the disciples. They grumbled that such wealth could have been given to the poor. Mark's gospel, which also describes the scene, offers a longer version of Jesus' response: *"Why are you bothering her? She has done a beautiful thing to me. The poor you will always have with you, and you can help them any time you want. But you will not always have me"* (Mark 14:6–7).

The point was that the disciples can and should always help the poor. In fact, in saying the poor will always be with us, Jesus was quoting from the Old Testament: *"There will always be poor people in the land. Therefore I command you to be openhanded toward your brothers and toward the poor and needy in your land"* (Deuteronomy 15:11).

And plenty of Jesus' other statements let us know that we must help the poor. After all, He began His public ministry in the gospel of Luke by reading from Isaiah 61: *"The Spirit of the Lord is on me, because he has anointed me to preach good news to the poor. He has sent me to proclaim freedom for the prisoners and recovery of sight for the blind, to release the oppressed, to proclaim the year of the Lord's favor"* (Luke 4:18–19).

In this, Jesus echoed many prophets, such as Amos, who delivered this word from the Lord: *"For three transgressions of Israel, and for four, I will not revoke the punishment, because they sell the righteous for silver, and the needy for a pair of sandals— those who trample the head of the poor into the dust of the earth, and turn aside the way of the afflicted"* (Amos 2:6–7 ESV).

Jesus made it clear in one of His last parables that our responses to the poor have eternal consequences. They are a matter of life and death. In Matthew 25, just before He was anointed in Bethany, Jesus said that at the last judgment, the King would welcome the righteous into His kingdom because "I was hungry and you gave me something to eat, I was thirsty and you gave me something to drink, I was a stranger and you invited me in, I needed clothes and you clothed me, I was sick and you looked after me, I was in prison and you came to visit me." When the righteous ask when they had ever done such things for Him, the King will answer, "I tell you the truth, whatever you did for one of the least of these brothers of mine, you did for me."

From beginning to end, the Bible implores Christians to care for the poor. How can American Christians help "the least of these" in the here and now? The next three chapters will grapple with this question. The answers might surprise you, and—if we are lucky—inspire you to action.

3. HOW CAN WE GIVE POOR KIDS A MILLION BUCKS?

"Being poor is having to live with choices you didn't know you made when you were 14 years old. Being poor is people who have never been poor wondering why you choose to be so."

—JOHN SCALZI

Delories Williams believed in discipline and getting things done. So much so that when she was out of earshot, some of her friends at Oakdale Covenant Church called her "Sarge."

For more than thirty years, Mrs. Williams, along with her friends Sethras Jones and Dorothy Shipp, ran the Academic Excellence program at Oakdale, a 1,200-member African-American congregation on Chicago's southwest side. Working out of a small office in the basement of the school next to the church, they marshaled an army of volunteers to tutor children, to run college-exam prep courses, and to walk parents and students through the college application and financial aid processes. With prayer, hard work, and an occasional bit of arm-twisting, they got almost every child from the church into college.

By the time Mrs. Williams died from ovarian cancer at seventy-four in the summer of 2007, she had helped hundreds of young people. At her memorial service, or "home-going," many of them stood up and testified about how Mrs. Williams transformed their lives. "People came up and told us that she was the reason they became a lawyer or a doctor or an accountant," says Catherine Gilliard, Mrs. Williams' daughter. "Everyone you met—they wanted to tell you a story about what my mother had done for them."

"My mother believed that education was the key to unlocking the future," Gilliard says. She was right. Any child who walked into the Academic Excellence ministry found hope, love, and the skills they needed to succeed. They walked out with their head held high and the chance to earn a million dollars. Almost two million, actually.

The median college graduate will earn $1,982,816 over a lifetime (see table 3.1). On the other hand, the median high school grad will earn $1,011,792, a difference of $971,024. For high school dropouts, the picture is even bleaker: They will earn on average $667,335 in a lifetime, or $1,315,481 less than a college grad.

Going to college, it turns out, is even better than winning the lottery.

| TABLE 3.1 | LIFETIME EARNINGS BY EDUCATION LEVEL |

EDUCATION LEVEL	Lifetime Earnings (Current Dollars)	Lifetime Earnings (Present Value)
Bachelor's Degree or More	$1,982,816	$563,516
High School Graduate	$1,011,792	$330,636
Less than High School	$667,335	$242,570
Differences:		
HS vs. Less than HS	$344,457	$88,066
College vs. HS	$971,024	$232,880
College vs. Less than HS	$1,315,481	$320,946

Calculations are based on the median income in 2005 for people with less than a high school education, people with a high school diploma but no college degree, and people with at least one college degree. The first column is the total dollars the median person in each category would earn between the ages of 15 and 65, assuming zero income while in school and ignoring pay increases due to future inflation or productivity growth. The second column is the present value of the lifetime stream of earnings, discounted at 5% per year, which is slightly larger than the inflation-adjusted average annual return on the S&P 500 Stock Index from 1950 to 2006.

Easy Money, the Powerball Way?

Don Harvey's semitruck had nearly two million miles on it by the time he returned home to Muldrow, Oklahom, from delivering a load of air conditioners to Madison, Wisconsin, in the summer of 2007. Right about the time he rolled into the driveway, the engine quit for good. Lucky for him, his wife, Joyce, had remembered to buy a Powerball ticket.

Earlier in the week, she had stopped by a Shell station in nearby Roland, Oklahoma, to pick one up. When she checked the winning numbers online, not long after Don arrived home, she broke down and cried, according to the Associated Press. The Harveys had won $105 million playing the lottery.

As well as things worked out for the Harveys, you might guess that the lottery is not the most efficient way to give someone a million dollars. The odds of the Harveys winning the Powerball, for example, were 176 million to one, Jim Scoggins, director of the Oklahoma Lottery commission, told the Associated Press.

And there aren't that many big winners in the lottery. Duane Burke, CEO of the Public Gaming Research Institute, said that in 1996, 1,136 people won a million dollars or more playing the lottery. Then again, in 1996 Americans also spent more than $34 billion on lottery tickets to produce those 1,136 million-dollar jackpots, which means that it cost an average of almost $30 million to give one person at least a million dollars. (Interestingly, the National Association of State and Provincial Lotteries, which supplied Burke's figures, claims that it has not collected data on million-dollar prize winners since 1996. They do, however, report that lottery sales topped $54 billion in 2005.)

Conversely, every college graduate has in effect won the lottery at a relatively cheap price—between $50,000 (at a four-year public institution) and $120,000 (at a four-year private college), according to the College Board.

Human Capital

Of all the questions raised in *Good Intentions*, this one seems the simplest: How do you give a poor kid a million dollars? You send them to college. But if education is so valuable, why do so few poor kids go to college?

Economists think of education as one component of something called "human capital." Usually, when economists talk about "capital," they mean things like buildings, machines, tools, and equipment. But people themselves grow and learn and develop "human capital" over time. Human capital is a product of our education, health, skills, and expertise—even our personal habits and values.

What might surprise most people is that the real wealth of developed nations such as the United States is found in human capital, according to Robert Fogel, the University of Chicago economic historian and cowinner of the 1993 Nobel prize in economics. In his book *The Fourth Great Awakening and the Future of Egalitarianism*, Fogel writes,

> The main form of capital today is not buildings, machines, or electric grids but labor skills, what economists call human capital or knowledge capital. Both for individuals and for businesses, it is the size and quality of these immaterial assets that determine success in competitive markets and conditions of life for ordinary people.

Fogel estimates that the value of human capital in the United States is about double the dollar value of all of the physical capital. This means that our human capital is worth more than twice as much as all of our skyscrapers and factories and houses and stores and cars and appliances and furniture—pretty much everything that we own, other than land.

And the way to give poor kids a million bucks is to help them develop *their* human capital, which is what Mrs. Williams and the other volunteers at Oakdale Covenant Church were doing in the 1970s, when they launched the Academic Excellence ministry. They were inspired by then-pastor Willie Jemison, who had led the church through a time of tremendous transition. In the 1960s, the Gresham neighborhood, where Oakdale is located, had been 95 percent white. The church, which had been founded by Swedish immigrants, had about two hundred people. By 1970, the neighborhood had become 95 percent African-American, and the church had shrunk to twenty-five people. Rather than close their doors, they called Rev. Jemison to be their pastor. He rebuilt the church into a congregation of more than twelve hundred.

But in the late 1970s, Pastor Jemison was worried. Too few children from the church went to college, and he thought that this would jeopardize their futures. While many church members valued education, few had college degrees. Mrs. Williams did—she had earned a degree in early childhood education while raising four children as a single mom and working full-time at the post office. "For as long as we could remember, Mom was taking a class," Catherine Gilliard remembers.

Mrs. Williams had also crossed racial lines. She moved her daughters from Altgeld Elementary on 71st and Loomis, an African-American school, to Foster Park Elementary on 85th and Wood, a school for white children (the *Brown v. Board of Education* decision had made school segregation illegal). She and the children would duck bottles and rocks being thrown by angry crowds who didn't want them in their neighborhood. A former soldier, Mrs. Williams was not going to let anyone stand in the way of her children getting the best possible education.

Pastor Jemison enlisted Mrs. Williams and several friends to form a scholarship committee, aimed at finding funds to help students pay for college. But that was not enough. They discovered that children at Oakdale, like many students from poor families, faced two obstacles when trying to get into college. The first was money. Not only did the students come from families with little money, but they attended overcrowded and under-funded schools.

It's a problem that remains to this day. In 2005, when the Education Trust studied school funding in forty-nine states, they found that the wealthiest school districts (those with the fewest poor students enrolled) spent on average $907 more each year per student than the poorest districts. In a class of twenty-five students, that's a difference of $22,675 per year. Things are even worse in Illinois, where the funding gap is $2,065 per year—or $51,625 for a class of twenty-five students. (New York had the worst funding gap: $2,280, or $57,000 a year for a class of twenty-five.) Having less money means schools often have poor facilities and less experienced teachers, and sometimes they even lack basic supplies.

The second obstacle came from a lack of what Robert Fogel calls "spiritual assets"—the intangible skills and abilities that are crucial to success. The students entering the Academic Excellence ministry often were missing those assets. They weren't prepared to take the SAT or ACT, exams essential for getting into college. They didn't know how to navigate the college application process or fill out financial aid forms. And many of the students did not believe that they could make it in college. This was especially true for students with so-so grades—kids who hadn't figured out how to thrive in school and didn't think they were college material.

"The smart kids with good grades had opportunities," Catherine Gilliard says. "Mom's focus was on the kids whose grades were 1.9 or 2.0—and who thought that this was all they would ever be capable of. She worked with them on their low self-esteem, and she made sure they got life skills along with academic skills."

To get students at Oakdale to aspire to college, Williams also organized visits to historically black colleges during spring break week. Each year, she would take as many as forty students on these college tours, which featured four or five separate schools. Every trip was different. Sometimes they would visit schools in Maryland; other times they would travel to colleges in North Carolina and Georgia. The trips allowed students to imagine what was possible for them. All of a sudden they were at schools where being an African-American college student was the norm—not the exception.

Today, many of the students with whom Mrs. Williams worked are professionals: doctors and lawyers, accountants and businesspeople. And their children have grown up and gone off to college on their own. It's with rare exception that a student will not go on to college, says D. Darrell Griffin, who succeeded Pastor Jemison in 2001. "It's just not tolerated around here."

Griffin says that on occasion, the Academic Excellence ministry worked "miracles." Over the course of thirty years, Mrs. Williams and other volunteers had developed close ties with college admissions officers and financial aid staff at a number of colleges, relationships they had nurtured over decades. Sometimes, their recommendation alone could get a student into college—even if that child had a poor academic record. If Mrs. Williams believed they had potential, she would not rest until she found a college for them.

"If a child has fallen through the cracks in terms of getting into school, the Academic Excellence ministry will use their network to get that child into school," Griffin says. "It's with rare, rare exception that a child who wants to go to school, regardless of their GPA, will not get in somewhere. And it has been the rare exception that they didn't get funded. The real strength of our ministry is this: If you can get us one parent or guardian involved, we can save that child."

Choices Good and Bad

Many efforts to reduce poverty—including Christian efforts—work on the assumption that being poor is a disease that
needs to be treated. And the symptoms of the poverty disease are
easy to identify: Because they make so little money, poor people
can't afford decent housing, can't pay for school lunches, can't
pay for health care, and so on. Consequently, most poverty-relief
programs tend to address the symptoms of poverty: raise the
minimum wage, provide food stamps and vouchers for housing,
and give poor kids a free lunch at school. These approaches make
it easier for poor people to get by. But they do not address the
causes of poverty.

Rather than seeing poverty as a disease, economists think of
poverty as an outcome of a decision-making process. This doesn't
mean that people choose to be poor; it means that people make
choices that are perfectly sensible in light of their circumstances
but that lead to poverty nonetheless.

Economists make three important assumptions about how
people make choices. First, people have their own *preferences*—
that is, they know what they like and don't like. Second, people
are *rational*. This doesn't mean that they make decisions that
other people think are logical. Instead, it means that people
pursue their goals the best way they know how. Third, people
face *constraints* that limit their choices. These are the obstacles
and hurdles that keep us from achieving our goals.

How do these three assumptions help us understand the
causes of poverty? It's safe to say that most poor people do not like
to be poor, which means that *preferences* are not the root cause of
poverty. Poor people are also *rational*: they know, in the same way
that rich people do, that when you are hungry, you need to eat.
When your job pays too little to live on, you seek a better job.
When your housing is unacceptable, you seek a better house.

The economist's third assumption about decision-making—

people face constraints that limit their choices—is really the key to understanding poverty. If poor people don't want to be poor, and if they know how to make good choices, then the most likely reason for their continued poverty is that their options are not very good.

Don and Joyce Harvey got lucky when they won the Powerball jackpot, and their monetary constraint all but went away. But the Oakdale Academic Excellence ministry was about knocking down constraints for every kid who walked through their door. Some of the constraints were due to a lack of information—knowing about different colleges and how to get into them. Other constraints were monetary—getting scholarships and other financial aid to pay the bill. And perhaps the most important constraints that Delories Williams knocked down were the kids' own lack of belief in themselves.

Building Spiritual Assets

The ministry at Oakdale specialized in developing spiritual and academic assets—realizing that without those intangibles, their students could not thrive in college or in life. This is the same conclusion a growing number of economists and researchers have reached. Robert Fogel, the Nobel laureate, says that in societies such as the United States, Canada, and Europe, "spiritual assets" are more important than money.

Fogel defines spiritual assets as "a sense of purpose, self-esteem, a sense of discipline, a vision of opportunity, and a thirst for knowledge," and he says that these assets play an enormous role in whether people succeed or fail. Without spiritual assets, poor families have a hard time making the kinds of choices that can transform their lives.

Fogel's ideas are echoed by James Heckman, another Nobel-prize-winning economist from the University of Chicago. Heckman's interest in poverty started out with studies of job-training programs for teenagers and GED programs. What he found surprised him. Publicly funded job-training programs didn't really work. They tried to cure "17 years of neglect" in a few months. According to Heckman, "Those who don't get those early skills are unlikely to benefit much from short-term public training programs later on."

And GED programs aren't any better. In one study, Heckman looked at the scores of soldiers taking the Armed Forces Qualifying Test. Those who had a GED—a General Equivalency Diploma earned by high school dropouts—did as well on the armed forces test as those who had graduated from high school. But GED holders earned less money than those high school graduates; they were more likely to be discharged for disciplinary reasons; and they had problems finishing basic training and/or college studies later on.

Despite their intelligence, the soldiers with a GED lacked "something," Heckman told the Federal Reserve Bank of Minneapolis in an interview. "They're missing motivation, self-control and forward-lookingness. I call these noncognitive skills." Such noncognitive skills, Heckman said, are "the key to explain[ing] success and failure in socioeconomic life."

One of the first places that these noncognitive skills (as Heckman calls them), or spiritual assets (as Fogel calls them), are important is in school. But not all students begin their academic careers on the same footing. Students from poor families often begin school at a deficit. They soon fall farther and farther behind students from wealthier families. It's as if the rich and middle-class kids' school backpacks come with extra provisions. Not only do they have pencils and paper, lunch boxes and sneakers, but they also come equipped with spiritual assets. Things like better vocabularies, self-confidence, and the ability to persevere when things go wrong, which make them ready to learn. In the language of economics, middle-class kids face fewer constraints.

In a November 2006 story titled "What It Takes to Make a

Student," Paul Tough, an editor at *The New York Times Sunday Magazine*, outlined some of the differences between rich and poor students. It turns out that middle-class parents and poor parents speak to their children in vastly disparate ways. The differences between the two groups were astonishing. "By age 3," Tough writes, "children whose parents were professionals had vocabularies of about 1,100 words, and children whose parents were on welfare had vocabularies of about 525 words. The children's I.Q.s correlated closely to their vocabularies. The average I.Q. among the professional children was 117, and the welfare children had an average I.Q. of 79."

Why such different results? It's not mere genetics. James Heckman points to research showing that early childhood interventions can actually increase poor children's IQs. So there is more going on than just smart parents begetting smart kids through DNA.

Researchers Betty Hart and Todd R. Risley found that parents who were professionals spoke to their children more and praised them more. Reporting on this study, Tough writes, "By age 3, the average child of a professional heard about 500,000 encouragements and 80,000 discouragements. For the welfare children, the situation was reversed: they heard, on average, about 75,000 encouragements and 200,000 discouragements."

The different parenting styles had profound effects on student IQs. More words and more affirmation meant a higher IQ. Fewer words and more discouragement led to lower IQs. As Tough puts it, "The professional parents were giving their children an advantage with every word they spoke, and the advantage just kept building up."

Having started ahead, students from middle-class families use their spiritual assets to accumulate even more spiritual assets. "A large body of research in social science, psychology and neuroscience shows that skill begets skill; that learning begets learning," Heckman says.

There is also substantial evidence of critical or sensitive periods in the lives of young children. Environments that do not cultivate both cognitive and noncognitive abilities (such as motivation, perseverance, and self-restraint) place children at an early disadvantage. Once a child falls behind in these fundamental skills, he is likely to remain behind.

Why do spiritual assets matter so much? Because they lead to opportunities and choices, argues Fogel. And opportunity and choice are the way most people improve their lives. In developed countries such as the United States, most people have access to the basics of life. Almost all of us have enough food to eat, clean water, access to education, shelter, electricity—and even cars, televisions, phones, and air-conditioning. Not all of these material assets are distributed evenly. But compared to most people in the world, and most Americans living in any other time, even the poorest American is extravagantly wealthy.

However, there is a great divide between rich and poor when it comes to choices and opportunity. And in a developed country such as the United States, that's what matters most.

"The quality of the choices and the range of opportunity depend critically on how well-endowed an individual is with spiritual resources," says Fogel.

> The quest for spiritual equity thus turns not so much on money as on access to spiritual assets, most of which are transferred and developed privately rather than through the market. Moreover, some of the most critical spiritual assets, such as a sense of purpose, self-esteem, a sense of discipline, a vision of opportunity, and a thirst for knowledge, are transferred at very young ages.

Without spiritual assets, poorer Americans become "spiritually estranged," as Fogel puts it, cut off and left behind the rest of American society. They have few options or opportunities to change their lives. "In America, poverty means having no choices," says Jim Sundholm, a longtime urban pastor and director of Covenant World Relief.

You Can't Stop Dreaming or You Start to Die

A lack of choices explains, in part, why so many poor people were stuck in New Orleans during Hurricane Katrina—they had no place left to go.

Before the levees broke, Cindy Cole had made a life for herself in the city's Ninth Ward. A single mom in her early twenties, Cole rented a small house for about $275, with plenty of relatives nearby to help care for her three children. But she had no job, no savings, and no options when the levee broke. Her house—and her whole way of life—was washed away. When Shaila Dewan of *The New York Times* caught up with Cole in July of 2007, she was stranded in Convent, Louisiana: a Katrina refugee, seemingly caught in limbo.

"This was not how Cindy Cole pictured her life at 26: living in a mobile home park called Sugar Hill, wedged amid the refineries and cane fields of tiny St. James Parish, 18 miles from the nearest supermarket," Dewan wrote. "Sustaining three small children on nothing but food stamps, with no playground, no security guards and nowhere to go."

JoAnn Anderson, another Katrina refugee in limbo, now living in Memphis, had rented half of a duplex in the Ninth Ward for twenty-two years while working as a housekeeper in New Orleans hotels. Now in her fifties, she was at least getting by before Katrina. "I was born poor; I'm probably going to die poor; and before the storm came through I was doing pretty good," Anderson told the *Times*.

As long as the levees held, Cole and Anderson were making it. But they were trapped as well. Their way of life, and the way of life for thousands of poor New Orleans residents, was fragile and could not withstand the floodwaters of Katrina.

Not long after the hurricane, writer and blogger John Scalzi, who had grown up poor and was the first person in his family to graduate from high school, posted a long essay called "Being Poor." It became one of the most linked-to essays on the Internet and began with "Being poor is knowing exactly how much everything costs." It ended with this:

> Being poor is knowing how hard it is to stop being poor.
>
> Being poor is seeing how few options you have.
>
> Being poor is running in place.
>
> Being poor is people wondering why you didn't leave.

Journalist John W. Fountain describes the same feeling of being trapped in poverty in his memoir, *True Vine*. Fountain grew up on Chicago's West Side in the North Lawndale neighborhood referred to as K-Town. (Most of the north-south streets in the neighborhood begin with the letter "K.") When he was a boy, the *Chicago Tribune* ran a long series on his community, known as the "Millstone series," describing residents as a permanent underclass that "devours every effort aimed at solving its problems."

Describing his childhood in *Illinois Matters* magazine, Fountain writes,

> I hated poverty. I hated the explosion of gunshots that cracked the still quiet of night and that seemed as inevitable as the rumble and rickety-click of a train passing over steel tracks somewhere in the distance. I hated the debilitating combination of poverty and hopelessness so evident in the winos that sipped spirits outside liquor stores down on 16th Street and in the people I knew who had long given up on life.

Despite being a gifted student, Fountain struggled to escape the poverty that had trapped many of his friends in K-Town. He grew up in a single-parent family—his dad had abandoned the family not long after Fountain was born. Fountain earned a scholarship at the University of Illinois at Urbana-Champaign but dropped out after his freshman year. His margin of error was so slim that an unpaid $700 tuition bill had unraveled his college dreams. By the time he was twenty-three, Fountain was married, had three children, and was living on welfare, with hardly enough money to buy shoes for his daughters. He found his way back up and out of the neighborhood, sustained in great part by the prayers of the older women of True Vine, a storefront church founded by his grandfather.

In his memoir, Fountain recalls the time he hit rock bottom. Sitting and talking with his grandmother, Fountain began to weep. There were too many obstacles, and the way out seemed too steep. "Grandmother, I just give up," Fountain told her. "I ain't even got no dreams no more. I give up, I just give up."

"This time Grandmother did not offer to pray or break into a sanctified praise," Fountain writes in *True Vine*.

> She did not scold or even offer a dry shoulder. She did not speak in tongues or moan in the spirit. She spoke simple words that struck me in a way that few ever have. "Wait a minute now, you can't stop dreamin' or you start to die," she said, her words half sung. "Oh no, baby darlin'. You can't stop dreamin'."

Fountain illuminates just how hard it is to stop being poor. Success in life, for anyone, is like climbing a mountain. Children from wealthier families start out with all the right equipment: hiking boots, safety ropes, pitons, an ice ax for climbing the snow and ice at the top, a sleeping bag and tent, and maybe even an oxygen canister and mask for when the air is thin. The climb is still hard, but they have the right tools and resources—the right spiritual assets.

People from poor families often climb without any gear at all. And it's a long way down when they fall. This is not because the poor are morally deficient or deserve to be poor. Rather, without the right skills and tools, the climb can be just too hard. Fountain's grandmother's advice on dreaming was a critical spiritual asset that she was able to pass on to him when he needed it most—and when he recognized that he needed it.

Not long after writing the "Being Poor" essay, John Scalzi was asked to give advice to people trying to get out of poverty. His first suggestion? Get an education. Then he added, "Learn patience. Anything is possible." But there will be many obstacles.

"Your plans will be thwarted by a bad alternator, an unreliable babysitter, an unexpectedly large electric bill, a fractured wrist and always by the fact that you don't have the money that allows other people to consider potholes what you see as a sinkhole that will rob you of your forward momentum," he wrote.

It is not easy to stop being poor, which is something people who are not poor seem to have a genuinely difficult time understanding. It's an uphill walk, and a bunch of crap is rushing downhill at you. You will avoid some of this crap, if you're smart. You will almost certainly not avoid it all. And some of what you won't avoid is going to carry you quite a distance back down the hill.

The Least of These . . .

So what can individual Christians or congregations do to help families and children develop the spiritual assets they need to thrive?

One of the best ways, according to economist James Heckman, is through high-quality preschool programs—both government-funded and privately run. This is because, as Robert Fogel puts it, "some of the most critical spiritual assets, such as a sense of purpose, self-esteem, a sense of discipline, a vision of opportunity, and a thirst for knowledge, are transferred at very young ages."

In an article coproduced by the Ounce of Prevention Fund, Heckman made an impassioned plea for expanding preschool programs—not just because it's the right thing to do from a social justice standpoint, but because they work.

"The best evidence suggests that learning begets learning, that early investments in learning are effective," he writes.

As a society, we cannot afford to postpone investing in children until they become adults, nor can we wait until they reach school age—a time when it may be too late to intervene. Since learning is a dynamic process, it is most effective when it begins at a young age and continues through adulthood. The returns to human capital investments are greatest for the young for two reasons: (a) skill begets skill, and (b) younger persons have a longer horizon over which to recoup the fruits of their investments.

Then he adds:

Children are born "ready to learn," but we must also attend to their social and emotional development. I am puzzled why we are taking such a narrow stance in this country toward preparing children for school and not thinking more clearly and more broadly about preparing them for life. We cannot prepare children to be ready for third grade by treating 2- and 3-year-olds like third graders. Rather, we need to help people see that children need an emotional and intellectual grounding to be able to think deeply and creatively about new ways to relate to each other, the world around them, and to have the confidence to act upon these thoughts.

Unlocking the Church Basement

America's true wealth is in its human capital, and unequal ownership of spiritual assets may be the most glaring human-capital disparity between rich and poor. The biggest hurdle to breaking poverty in America is finding ways to transfer spiritual assets to those who lack them. This is much harder than transferring material assets.

Transferring spiritual assets requires time—the time of a person rich in spiritual assets spent with a person poor in them. As Heckman's research shows, the younger the recipient of such time, the more effective it is.

Many churches use their children's facilities as preschools during the week. Yet all across the country, there are church basements that are locked up all week long. Basements that could house preschool programs for poor kids. Basements that could house low-cost private schools that would offer poor kids a path out of low-quality, underfunded public schools that are failing. Basements that could house Academic Excellence programs for teenagers, such as the one that Delories Williams started. Basements that could do wonders for "the least of these."

Fogel suggests that churches put their basements and other empty facilities, such as Sunday school classrooms, to work, helping children build human capital. "Another program targeting very young children involves the expansion and spiritual enrichment of nursery and day-care programs," he writes. "One aspect of this expansion should be the encouragement of houses of worship to convert basements and other unused facilities into space suitable for nursery programs."

Most importantly, churches can provide hope. This was something that Delories Williams never forgot. She spent the last few weeks of her life in the hospital, when the cancer made her too weak to stay at home. Even from her hospital bed, she kept busy, making calls to colleges and checking up on her students, making the most of every moment. When she was no longer able to speak, she passed notes to her friend Sethras Jones with names of students to follow up on.

What kept her going? Her undying faith in Jesus and her

belief that education could help save young people, no matter what their circumstances. And then there were the miracles.

Not long before she died, Mrs. Williams had seen another one, as Joy Dillard, an eighteen-year veteran of the Academic Excellence ministry recalled while sitting with a group of Oakdale volunteers and college students.

"I do know firsthand that she could work miracles," Dillard said. "My son, in his junior year, started bringing one of his friends from high school to Oakdale. And his friend eventually joined. I loved him to death but I knew that no college was going to accept him."

But Mrs. Williams knew better. She helped the young man with his college applications, and pushed him to rewrite his application essay over and over until it was nearly perfect. He eventually enrolled in Alabama A&M University and is on schedule to graduate on time.

But that's not all, Dillard said.

He called this summer and asked for some information, because he was thinking about applying to law school. This was a boy who we thought was not going to be able to get into any college. She got him into that college. He stayed—money was always an issue but he made it through—and now he's talking about going to law school. That was Mrs. Williams in action. It's one more life that has been saved.

4. MUST THE POOR
ALWAYS BE WITH US?

Poverty in America

It was July 1932. The unemployment rate was nearly 24 percent. United States economic output was in a free fall—real gross domestic product in 1932 was only three-fourths of what it had been three years earlier. Breadlines and soup kitchens were commonplace. More than ten thousand banks had failed. Millions of Americans fell into desperate poverty, seemingly overnight.

Even before the Great Depression hit, most middle-class Americans were already poor, as Matt Bai reported in a story for *The New York Times Magazine*'s "money issue" in 2007. "According to the economists Thomas Piketty and Emmanuel Saez," Bai wrote, "the average income of an American taxpayer in 1929, using today's dollars, was about $16,000 a year; the entire middle class, in other words, was poor by modern standards."

At the Democratic Party's national convention, Franklin Delano Roosevelt, the governor of New York, accepted the party's presidential nomination. Roosevelt spoke in religious terms about unseating the Republican Party:

Let us be frank in acknowledgment of the truth that many amongst us have made obeisance to Mammon, that the profits of speculation, the easy road without toil, have lured us from the old barricades. To return to higher standards we must abandon the false prophets and seek new leaders of our own choosing.

Roosevelt then pledged to bring America back to prosperity and a more equal distribution of wealth. "This is more than a political campaign; it is a call to arms," he said. "Give me your help, not to win votes alone, but to win in this crusade to restore America to its own people."

Of course, Roosevelt won the 1932 election and launched the "New Deal" over the next several years. This included Social Security's retirement benefits, the cash transfers of Aid to Dependent Children (later renamed Aid to Families with Dependent Children, or AFDC), and a minimum wage of twenty-five cents an hour. Another New Deal program, aimed at providing job training to young workers, was the National Youth Association (NYA). In 1935, the Texas branch of the NYA hired a twenty-six-year-old as state director. His name was Lyndon B. Johnson.

Many of the New Deal reforms became permanent parts of American society. World War II came and went, and the United States enjoyed unprecedented economic prosperity. Still, by 1964, when Lyndon Johnson became president, the problem of poverty persisted. Nearly one American in five was living below a newly defined "poverty line." At that time, Bai reported, there were still rural communities in the United States with "no electricity, no running water, no primary-school education." The poor were still with us. The New Deal had not been enough.

So in his first State of the Union address on January 8, 1964, President Johnson declared an "unconditional war on poverty in America." The weapons in Johnson's war on poverty emerged over the next several years: improved educational opportunities for poor people, including Head Start for preschoolers; food stamps for poor families; school nutrition programs for children; improved Social Security benefits for the elderly poor; and a variety of job-training programs for youths and adults.

When Johnson launched his antipoverty offensive, the percentage of poor people in the United States was already in decline. The poverty line is based on family income and family size: In 2006, for example, the poverty-line income for a traditional family of four was $20,444; for a single head of household with four minor children, the poverty line income was $24,059. According to the Census Bureau, more than 22 percent of Americans lived below the poverty line in 1959. By 1969, that figure had dropped to 12 percent. It has fluctuated between 11 and 15 percent ever since, with the rate highest during the 1980s and early 1990s (See figure 4.1).

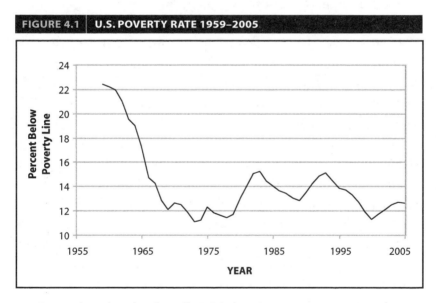

Source: based on data from the US Census Bureau.

When poverty persisted, even after the New Deal and War on Poverty—both launched by the Democratic Party—Republicans went on a counteroffensive. They blamed persistent poverty on welfare—specifically, Aid for Families with Dependent Children (AFDC), which they believed rewarded poor people, in particular, poor women, for behaving badly. In the 1994 elections, the Republican Party took control of both houses of Congress, spurred by the party's "Contract with America." One key component of this contract was welfare reform, based on the belief that welfare encouraged teen pregnancy while discouraging marriage and work.

In 1996, the Republican Congress and Democratic President, Bill Clinton, passed a broad welfare-reform law that replaced AFDC with a new program called Temporary Assistance for Needy Families (TANF). TANF gave states broad flexibility in how to administer their welfare programs, though it placed a five-year lifetime eligibility cap on participants' receipt of federal funds and imposed work requirements on recipients.

As figure 4.1 shows, when welfare reform was passed in 1996, the poverty rate was already declining. Welfare caseloads were on the decline as well, and the declines continued until the 2001 recession. Since 2002, welfare caseloads have fallen a little bit more. Still, somewhere around 12 percent of Americans live below the poverty line.

The New Deal and the Contract with America reveal a deep divide among Americans on how to best help poor people escape poverty. The divide dates back to the Poor Laws first passed in Elizabethan England, which split poor people into two camps. The *deserving poor*—the old, the sick, along with widows, orphans, and other destitute children—were treated with compassion. They sometimes received "outdoor assistance"—free food, clothes, and other basic necessities—or were sent to live with wealthier families for a short period of time. In other cases, poor families received "indoor assistance" and went to live in poorhouses and other institutions. (Some poor children were treated less charitably and auctioned off to serve as cheap labor for farmers.) The deserving poor were seen primarily as *victims*. It was believed that, with enough assistance, they could get back on their feet and pull themselves out of poverty.

The *undeserving poor*, those without jobs who were healthy enough to work, were punished for their poverty. Seen as shiftless, lazy drunkards—and immoral—they were rounded up into almshouses or debtor's prisons and set to work. Unless they changed their ways, these undeserving poor would always be poor, or so most of society believed at the time.

The earliest American colonists approached the poor from both of these perspectives. In the 1600s, they gave outdoor relief *and* built poorhouses. Since that time, Americans have pingponged between two extremes—first treating the poor as victims, then as sinners. But neither approach has solved the problem of poverty over the long term, as Susan E. Mayer, a professor at the University of Chicago, points out. In recounting the history of poverty relief in the United States, Mayer draws on Grace Abbot's 1941 book *From Relief to Social Security.* "We have proceeded along in a stumbling fashion," Abbot wrote, "trying one method of care after another, and often moving from bad to worse, and back again, in search for a 'cure of pauperism.'"

Neither approach worked because both merely treated the *symptoms* of poverty. Neither helped poor people build the human capital or develop the spiritual assets needed to pull themselves out of poverty.

In chapter 3, we discussed how to address the causes of poverty. However, effective solutions take a long time to work, and in the meantime, people are suffering. So what can Christians do to relieve some of the present suffering while working on long-term solutions?

Would Jesus Vote for Food Stamps?

One response is to support federal policies aimed at assisting the poor. Such policies take three basic forms:

• *Social insurance*, such as Social Security and Medicare, covers everyone, regardless of wealth or income. These programs provide income and health benefits for the elderly. Social Security payments have been effective in reducing poverty among the elderly. And Medicare reduces the amount the elderly spend from their own pockets on healthcare, which effectively increases their standard of living by freeing up money to spend on other things. As a result, Social Security and Medicare have helped relieve poverty among the elderly.

• *Cash transfer programs* give money directly to poor people. These include Temporary Aid to Needy Families (TANF) and the Earned Income Tax Credit (EITC).

• *In-kind transfer programs* give material assistance to poor people. Examples are food stamps, Medicaid, housing assistance, school-nutrition programs, and aid to Women, Infants, and Children (WIC).

Much of this is done for surprisingly little money. Table 4.1 shows federal spending for antipoverty programs in 2002. Food stamps, for example, cost $20 billion. That's less than $70 per American—a fairly small expense to make sure that no children go hungry. And WIC—which provides things like milk, formula, and baby food to poor moms and children—costs $5 billion, or $17 per American.

The most expensive social welfare program is Medicaid, which costs $270 billion to cover about twenty-four million Americans. That spending reflects the same skyrocketing health care costs affecting all Americans. For comparison purposes, the military budget in 2002 was $316 billion out of a total budget of almost $2 trillion—that does not include additional spending for the war in Iraq. Social Security was $432 billion; Medicare was $241 billion.

TABLE 4.1	FEDERAL EXPENDITURES ON SOCIAL WELFARE PROGRAMS IN 2002
Program Name	Dollars Spent (Billions)
Cash Transfer Programs:	
Temporary Aid to Needy Families	16
Earned Income Tax Credit	32
In-Kind Transfer Programs:	
Food Stamps	20
Medicaid	270
Housing Assistance	22
School Lunch	6
Women, Infants, and Children	5

Source: Bradley R. Schiller, *The Economics of Poverty and Discrimination*, 9th Ed., 2004.

Social welfare programs have been very effective in relieving the symptoms of poverty. They make it easier for the poor to get by. They don't, however, lift people out of poverty, because they don't address poverty's causes. That is, they don't build human capital, and they don't transfer spiritual assets.

Many programs have also created some perverse incentives. For example, AFDC/TANF payments drop as a person earns more. So a person's take-home pay for working another hour is cut when their benefits drop. Here's how it works: Say a working mom earns $8 an hour for forty hours a week, or $320 a week in cash; for making that money, she might lose $200 worth of benefits from TANF, food stamps, Medicaid, and so on. If this is indeed the case, her net gain for those forty hours of hard labor would only be $120—or $3 an hour—and she would probably pay more than that for child care. Consequently, this particular working mother would actually be better off quitting her job and staying at home.

Also, since benefits are determined by household income, having an intact family—with both a working father and a working mother present—means fewer benefits. There are other consequences of even greater significance to family stability. Single mothers with access to welfare payments, food stamps, subsidized housing, free school breakfast and lunch, Medicaid, and so on are likely to form their own households rather than live with extended family. And this decision is very likely to result in a household living below the poverty line for a long, long time.

It's not clear whether the 1996 welfare reforms have helped. The most significant reform was a five-year time limit on TANF payments. The reforms required benefits recipients to seek work in order to stay eligible. What happened after the reforms?

Welfare caseloads fell after the 1996 reforms—but they had already started dropping in 1993, three years before welfare reform took effect. It is hard to tell how much of the reduction in welfare caseloads was due to the reforms. Recent research suggests that welfare recipients are more likely to be working now than before the reforms. Whether they are actually better off, however, remains unclear.

The Earned Income Tax Credit (EITC), on the other hand, has been much more effective. First enacted in 1975, the EITC gives poor taxpayers a tax credit for each dollar they make. The credit rate is as high as forty cents for every dollar earned by parents with at least two children. The EITC is also refundable—if a poor family doesn't owe any income taxes, they get a check for the whole tax credit. In general, the EITC has been successful in helping families out of poverty because it encourages work and puts cash in their hands as an incentive.

According to the IRS, twenty-two million tax payers received EITCs in 2005—a total of $41.4 billion. In 2007, the EITC was worth as much as $4,500. Unfortunately, according to the IRS, one in four people who are eligible for the EITC don't claim it. Efforts to expand the scope of the EITC—and to make sure that everyone who is eligible receives the credit—will also help reduce poverty.

Is the Living Wage a Biblical Mandate?

Another common response to alleviating the symptoms of poverty has been to support a mandatory "living wage," or at least a higher minimum wage. In July 2007, that support became reality when a new federal minimum wage went into effect, going up from $5.15 to $5.85 per hour. The increase will be phased in over two years, so that by July 2009, the minimum wage will reach $7.25.

Now, almost no one can live on $5.15 an hour. Working at this wage for forty hours a week for fifty-two weeks means an annual income of $10,712. At $7.25 per hour, that total jumps to $15,080. Neither of these amounts is enough for most Americans to live on. That's led a number of community activists and Christian leaders to push for a "living wage"—something closer to $10 or even $14 an hour.

One major supporter of a living wage is the interfaith group Let Justice Roll. (The group's name comes from Amos 5:24: "But let justice roll on like a river, righteousness like a never-failing stream!") Members include the National Council of Churches, the Episcopal Church USA, the Presbyterian Church USA, the Evangelical Lutheran Church in America, the American Baptist Churches USA, and the United Methodist Church; numerous interfaith groups; several Catholic social agencies; Jim Wallis's Sojourners/Call to Renewal; and even the Baylor University Students for Social Justice.

Let Justice Roll's beliefs are clear:

Wages are a bedrock moral issue. Wages reflect our personal values and our nation's values. Wages reflect whether we believe workers are just another cost of business—like rent, electricity, or raw materials—or human beings with inherent dignity, human rights, and basic needs such as food, shelter, and health care. The minimum wage is where society draws the line: This low and no lower. Our bottom line is this: A job should keep you out of poverty, not keep you in it.

Based on this bottom line, Let Justice Roll has advocated higher minimum wages at both the federal level and in various states. According to the Rev. Dr. Nancy Jo Kemper, a Let Justice Roll steering committee member and executive director of the Kentucky Council of Churches, "The minimum wage is not just a matter of economics, but it is a values issue."

This is true. Deciding the smallest amount a person ought to be paid for an hour of work is a moral issue. But even though the minimum wage is not *just* a matter of economics, it *is* a matter of economics.

Economists have no special ability or training to help them decide the moral question, but they can certainly tell us what the real-world effects of minimum-wage hikes are. And it turns out that when the minimum wage goes up, poverty doesn't necessarily go down. To understand why, let's look at how labor markets work.

Workers get jobs because they need money. Their most basic goal is to get the highest pay possible for the number of hours they are willing to work. If they find a better job, they take it.

They try to maximize the benefits—money, working conditions, job satisfaction, and meaning—of their job.

Employers do the same thing. They do not hire workers because the workers need money. Employers hire workers because customers want the product those workers make. When the customers buy the product, the employer makes money. The amount employers can pay workers is limited by two factors: the price customers are willing to pay and all the other costs of making the product—including rent, utilities, materials, equipment, debt, and much more. In other words, employers face scarcity. There are outside limits on what they can pay workers.

The employer also wants to earn enough profit to make the

business worthwhile. If a business loses money or makes little profit, the owners will shut it down and use their resources to do something else—just as workers will take better jobs if they can. When wages surpass these outside limits and make the business unprofitable, employers won't keep it open.

These limits also affect the number of hours an employer can afford. If wages go up, the limits induce an employer to do one of three things. They either hire fewer workers (or fire some), reduce the hours of their current workers, or buy machines to replace workers. Decades of studies on the effects of the minimum wage confirm this: Small increases in the minimum wage lead to small reductions in employment of low-skilled workers, especially workers who are young, black, and/or less-educated.

Surprisingly, increases in the minimum wage do not make much difference in overall poverty rates. A higher minimum wage helps some poor workers; they end up with more money. But it hurts other poor workers—those who lose their jobs or never get hired in the first place. The poor workers without jobs lose money, while the ones who keep jobs earn more. In effect, a higher minimum wage transfers money from one set of poor people to another.

There is another important unintended consequence of a minimum-wage hike. When minimum wages go up, poor high school kids who are so-so students—the kinds of kids that Delories Williams managed to get into college in chapter 3—are more likely to drop out to seek a job. Unfortunately, because they have limited human capital, and jobs for low-skilled workers are scarcer, they are less likely to find a job. Now they face a double whammy. Because they dropped out, they aren't building human capital at school. And because they can't get a job, they aren't building human capital through work experience. Besides that, they don't have any money.

So why do so many people want to increase the minimum wage if it has these effects?

Believing that "a job should keep you out of poverty, not keep you in it" sounds moral. It is a good intention. But raising the minimum wage is not the best way to make that belief a reality.

It is not the best way to keep people out of poverty.

Robert Reich, who was Secretary of Labor under President Clinton, admitted as much to *The New York Times*. Reich told the *Times* that, when it comes to fighting poverty, the minimum wage doesn't work as well as the Earned Income Tax Credit. On the other hand, Reich argued that raising the minimum wage has "a powerful moral and political impact" at a time when there is great anxiety among U.S. workers.

"They see neighbors and friends being fired for no reason by profitable companies, executives making off like bandits while thousands of their own workers are being laid off," Reich told the *Times*. "They see health insurance drying up, employer pensions shrinking. Promises to retirees of health benefits are simply thrown overboard. The whole system has aspects that seem grossly immoral to average working people." Instead of fighting poverty, Reich added, the minimum wage "demarcates our concept of decency with regard to work."

Is there any justification for a minimum wage, then? Certainly, our society can make the moral decision that work should pay at least a certain amount if someone is to do it. But such moral judgments should contemplate the cost of lost jobs, declining educational attainment of poor students, and the limited effects on overall poverty that minimum-wage hikes have before concluding that a "living wage" must be paid to all workers.

Advocating for a living wage feels good because it punishes the sins of employers. As Reich put it, many Americans feel that employers have violated "a social contract" by chasing profits at the expense of the workers. Raising the minimum wage seems easy, because it makes employers spend more on their workers instead of hoarding profits for themselves.

But as we've seen, higher minimum wages don't hurt employers very much. Instead, the higher pay comes out of the pockets of other poor people—those who lose or can't find jobs. The EITC, on the other hand, does a better job of keeping working people out of poverty. Unlike the minimum wage, the EITC focuses solely on the poor. (After all, not every minimum-wage worker is poor; many are middle-class teenagers earning spending money.)

And the EITC spreads the cost across all taxpayers, not just the poor. Advocating for increases in the scope of the EITC, and helping everyone who is eligible take advantage of it, is a better way to let justice roll.

A High-Stakes Failure

In chapter 3, we learned that human capital is the best long-term solution to poverty. And one of the best ways to build human capital is to improve schools.

Some conservatives have seized on this idea and come up with the perfect weapon to improve public schools—high-stakes testing. The idea is simple. If schools are held accountable for their students' performance, they will work harder to improve the education they offer.

High-stakes testing is at the heart of the federal "No Child Left Behind" legislation, in place since 2002. The "big idea" behind the legislation was that every child in the United States should be proficient in math and reading by 2014. And one important way to carry out the big idea was to hold schools accountable through yearly tests. If too many students failed the tests, schools would be punished. Administrators and teachers could lose their jobs, and the schools' funding could be cut.

No Child Left Behind was modeled mainly after the back-to-basics approach used by the Houston Independent School District in the 1990s. During that time, a number of schools in impoverished neighborhoods began to outperform schools from wealthy suburbs. One of those schools was Wesley Elementary School, where almost 80 percent of the students were poor. Students were drilled in the basics constantly, and teachers whose classes didn't perform were let go.

By 2003, as *The Dallas Morning News* reported, "Wesley rocketed to the top of the state in reading. It finished No. 1 in third grade out of 3,155 schools." The school's fourth graders finished fourth in the state; the fifth graders finished seventh. Unfortunately, the *Morning News* also reported that "all three groups of kids saw major drops in scores the next year."

Despite the subsequent drops in scores, the techniques used at Wesley spread throughout the city and across the state, setting off what was known as "the Texas miracle" in education. That success catapulted Rod Paige, superintendent of Houston schools, into President George W. Bush's cabinet as his first-term Secretary of Education. It also inspired No Child Left Behind.

But by 2005, the Texas miracle had begun to unravel. On March 31 of that year, the *Morning News* reported suspicious test results at nearly four hundred Texas schools. A subsequent investigation found widespread cheating. The high-stakes testing had, perversely, proved the perfect incentive for cheating. Troubled schools with high numbers of poor students got little money to improve their programs. If too many of their students failed the state test, teachers and administrators could be fired. So a sizable number of them cheated—either by giving answers to students or by manipulating the state's reporting procedures.

In 2002, Austin High School in Houston was named an exemplary school by the state of Texas for its academic performance. The school had achieved that status by under reporting the number of students who dropped out. As *The New York Times* reported, "during a decade in which, routinely, as many as half of Austin students failed to graduate, the school's reported dropout rate fell from 14.4 percent to 0.3 percent."

At Sharpstown High, officials reportedly held back troubled students in the ninth grade so their test results would not reflect poorly on the school. "The secret of doing well in the 10th-grade tests is not to let the problem kids get to the 10th grade," former associate principal Robert Kimball told the *Times*.

The Texas testing reforms provided an incentive to increase test scores. What differed by school was the constraints on getting higher scores. At well-off schools with high-achieving students, good test scores were easiest to achieve by making sure the kids were ready for the test and letting them do well. But in schools where students lacked basic spiritual assets and had a history of low educational achievement, it was actually easier to get test scores up by cheating than by honest means. The biggest miracle is that enough teachers and administrators were innately honest that cheating wasn't more common—a testament to the educators' spiritual assets.

Blatant cheating isn't the only way around the testing rules of No Child Left Behind. When too many students in states like California, Ohio, Mississippi, and Texas didn't score well enough to pass the mandated tests, those states took advantage of a loophole in the law allowing states to define "proficiency" for themselves. When not enough students scored high enough to be "proficient," these states either made the test easier or lowered the percentage of correct answers required to be "proficient."

"It took state governments a couple of years to realize just what that meant, but now they have caught on—and many of them are engaged in an ignoble competition to see which state can demand the least of its students," Paul Tough wrote in *The New York Times Sunday Magazine*.

> At the head of this pack right now is Mississippi, which has declared 89 percent of its fourth-grade students to be proficient readers, the highest percentage in the nation, while in fact, the

National Assessment of Educational Progress shows that only 18 percent of Mississippi fourth graders know how to read at an appropriate level—the second-lowest score of any state. In the past year, Arizona, Maryland, Ohio, North Dakota, and Idaho all followed Mississippi's lead and slashed their standards in order to allow themselves to label uneducated students educated.

It's hard enough for poor kids to get an education. The cheating and lowered standards that followed high-stakes testing made it worse—they sent a message that kids were learning what they needed, when most anyone could tell (most anyone other than those kids, anyway) that they weren't learning enough.

Result-Oriented Faith

The poor are still with us. Jesus wants His followers to be generous with the poor. But when it comes to advocating for public policies that help poor people, good intentions are not enough. As we've seen, Christians often peg their beliefs to specific policies—a living wage, high-stakes testing, expanded social welfare programs—without asking, "Do these ideas work?" They base their arguments on theology rather than evidence.

But as we learn from the parable of the Sheep and the Goats (Matthew 25:31–46), results matter. In that parable, the King does not say, "When I was hungry, you intended to feed me." He says, "When I was hungry, you gave me something to eat."

5. IS BONO RIGHT?

"Poverty is not just low GDP; it is dying babies, starving children, and oppression of women and the downtrodden."

—WILLIAM EASTERLY

Where the Streets Have No Name

In 1985, not long after performing in the Live Aid concert, which raised more than $200 million for famine relief in Africa, the Irish rock star Bono and his wife, Ali, traveled to Ethiopia. There they spent five weeks working with the Christian charity World Vision at an orphanage and food-distribution program. The lead singer of U2 wanted to find out about poverty and famine firsthand. What he saw seemed beyond belief: a nation of proud, almost regal people reduced to absolute, wretched poverty. In recalling that trip, Bono told Brian Williams of *NBC News* about "waking up in northern Ethiopia and mist leaving the ground and watching people coming, walking all through the night, coming, thousands of them coming to a feeding station to beg for food—to beg for their lives."

When it came time to leave, Bono told Ali that he would never forget what he had seen in Ethiopia. "Of course you'll forget," she replied.

She was right. There are some problems too big even for a rock star to solve. Despite his best intentions, the challenge of poverty in Africa was something the then-twentysomething Bono was not ready to grapple with. So Bono went back to "life as normal" in the developed world. He lost himself in work and family, putting thoughts of Ethiopia out of his mind.

Like many Christians who try to address global poverty, Bono realized that the problems poor people face appear insurmountable. A billion people live on less than one dollar a day. Many governments and economies in poor countries are in shambles. AIDS, famine, malaria, contaminated drinking water, and disease conspire to kill millions each year. According to a report from the World Health Organization, twenty-two thousand people die each day from poverty-related causes, most of which are preventable.

People living on less than a dollar a day suffer from "extreme poverty." They miss more meals than they eat and live in ramshackle housing—without even the basics of a roof and a chimney. They lack basic clothing items such as shoes, have no clean water or access to sanitation, and have little or no health care; their children rarely attend school at all; their babies die at dramatically high rates; and poor nutrition makes ten-year-old children as small as American seven-year-olds. Extreme poverty means that life is a daily struggle to survive, and too many lose the fight. As William Easterly, a former World Bank economist, describes it, poverty is "dying babies, starving children, and oppression of women and the downtrodden."

To put the numbers in perspective, consider this: In 1981, more than 1.4 billion people lived in extreme poverty (table 5.1). Since then, thanks mainly to the remarkable economic growth of China, India, and other Southeast Asian countries, more than 400 million people have been lifted from that misery. Left behind, however, are the "bottom billion"—a group more than three times the population of the United States, living in desperate, almost unspeakable conditions and with little hope of escape. One out of every six people in the world falls into this category.

TABLE 5.1	PEOPLE LIVING IN EXTREME POVERTY IN 1981 AND 2001 BY REGION OF WORLD			
	1981		**2001**	
Region	**Millions of People**	**Percentage of Population**	**Millions of People**	**Percentage of Population**
East Asia	795.6	57.7	271.3	14.9
South Asia	474.8	51.5	431.1	31.3
Sub-Saharan Africa	163.6	41.6	315.8	46.9
Latin America/Caribbean	35.6	9.7	49.8	9.5
Middle East/North Africa	9.1	5.1	7.1	2.4
Eastern Europe/Central Asia	3.1	0.7	17.6	3.7
World	1,481.8	40.4	1,092.7	21.1

Source: Shaohua Chen and Martin Ravallion, "How the World's Poorest Have Fared Since the Early 1980s," World Bank Policy Research Working Paper No. 3341, June 2004.

Unlike the rest of the world, things have gotten dramatically worse in sub-Saharan Africa, where the number of people living in extreme poverty has nearly doubled since 1981, and where war, famine, and AIDS claim millions of lives each year.

The Goal Is Elevation

In the 1990s, nearly a decade after his first trip to Africa, Bono began to see a ray of hope. When he learned that African nations were paying more than $250 million per month—more than had been raised at Live Aid—to repay loans to the world, he found a cause to believe in. Most of that loan money had been squandered by inept governments or stolen by kleptocratic leaders like Mobutu Sese Seko, who allegedly pocketed more than $5 billion during thirty years as president of what is now the Democratic Republic of Congo. If the burden of those loans could be lifted, and enough new aid money for relief and development could be spent in the developing world, then the bottom billion might stand a fighting chance.

That's the argument he made in 2004, while speaking to leaders of the British Labour Party, which included current prime minister Gordon Brown and former prime minister Tony

Blair. The plan was already working, Bono said. In Uganda, where debt had been cancelled, "three times as many children" were going to school. Still, more had to be done; so Bono asked the British government to "double aid, double its effectiveness, and double trouble for corrupt leaders" in Africa.

While speaking in the United States at the 2006 National Prayer Breakfast, Bono made an impassioned plea for what is known as the "ONE Campaign," which aspires to "make poverty history." Following up on debt relief pledged but not fully delivered by the G8 summit—a gathering of some of the wealthiest and most powerful countries in the world—the ONE Campaign wants the United States and other rich nations to spend an additional 1 percent of their national budgets to provide "clean water for all; school for every child; medicine for the afflicted, an end to extreme and senseless poverty."

"One percent is not merely a number on a balance sheet," Bono said.

> One percent is the girl in Africa who gets to go to school, thanks to you. One percent is the AIDS patient who gets her medicine, thanks to you. One percent is the African entrepreneur who can start a small family business, thanks to you. One percent is not redecorating presidential palaces or money flowing down a rat hole. This one percent is digging waterholes to provide clean water.

Bono made the same comments a few months later at a leadership conference sponsored by Willow Creek Community Church in Barrington, Illinois. After sharing the story of how he came to faith in Jesus, Bono said that he had experienced a second conversion while visiting Africa and seeing firsthand how poverty destroys people's lives. He asked the more than eight thousand leaders gathered at Willow Creek (and more than seventy thousand others who tuned in via satellite) to get their churches involved in ending "stupid poverty"—the kind that causes children to die from easily curable diseases.

So is Bono right? Can forgiving debt and the ONE Campaign save the bottom billion? And should Christians act to make these visions come true, to make extreme poverty "history"?

Grace . . . A Thought that Changed the World

Bono's Willow Creek remarks followed an address by Bill Hybels, the church's pastor. He told a story about a recent trip he had taken to a village in Zambia. Willow Creek feeds and educates about eleven hundred AIDS orphans in that village, so that at least in that one place "there are no AIDS orphans uncared for," Hybels said.

One day, Hybels met an old woman who was dragging a bag of "mealy-meal"—a life-sustaining maize product given out by the church. The woman was caring for two orphans, along with two of her grandchildren, and the five of them were dragging the bag along the road. Hybels offered to carry the bag to her home, which was about two miles away. During that journey, Hybels said that he had a moment of "penetrating clarity." When church leaders are faithful and effective, he said, when they preach the Word of God and help people come to faith and teach them that to be a follower of Jesus Christ means to have compassion for the poor and to care about widows and orphans, "then people live." If church leaders fail to do these things, "people die."

Realizing that God wants Christians to help the poor is one important step. As we noted in chapter 1, God created a world where there was enough for everyone. It's become clear that not everyone has enough—that enormous numbers of God's children do not have enough food, water, shelter, or medicine to survive.

How to change that is the hard part.

Sometimes You Can't Make It on Your Own

One step advocated by Jeffrey Sachs, an economist at Columbia University, is to forgive debts owed by governments in developing countries and substantially increase aid given to these same countries. Sachs has spent more than twenty years studying development in poor nations and advising governments in Poland, Bolivia, Russia, India, and China on economic issues. His work has inspired the kind of policies that Bono advocates—Bono even calls Sachs his "tutor."

In his book *The End of Poverty,* Sachs explains the scope of the problem. Back in the 1700s, everyone was poor. From Europe to India, Africa to Japan, almost everyone lived on a farm and barely eked out an existence. Wealth was consolidated in the hands of a few, and people hoped to live for forty years at best.

"Children died in vast numbers," Sachs writes. "Many waves of disease and epidemics, from the black death of Europe to smallpox and measles, regularly washed through society and killed mass numbers of people. Episodes of hunger and extreme weather and climatic fluctuations sent societies crashing."

Then, beginning around 1750, life began to change in some places. Western Europe, which had already benefited from such agricultural advances as crop rotation, experienced the Industrial Revolution. Beginning in England and spreading throughout Europe and the New World was what Sachs calls "The Great Transformation"—putting some countries on the road to developing technologically advanced and wealthy societies, while leaving others behind.

Those left behind are caught in what Sachs calls the "poverty trap." To develop a growing economy, people everywhere need to set aside part of their current incomes to invest in the future through better tools and equipment, medical treatments for better health, and education to increase future earnings. But the extremely poor have so few resources that everything they have and earn and produce is needed just to stay alive today. Nothing is left to invest for the future.

Without the ability to invest in the future, poor people—and poor nations—become trapped.

Of course, other factors interact with and reinforce the poverty trap, such as geographic and demographic realities, bad government, war, and cultural and political hurdles. To reduce extreme poverty, Sachs believes that economists must devise growth plans based on each country's particular circumstances and needs. Common features of these plans are debt forgiveness and large increases in grants to stabilize developing-country currencies and to build roads, water and sewage systems, health facilities, and schools. He advocates having the United Nations oversee the various agencies that administer aid to developing countries and get them all working together to end extreme poverty.

Sachs believes that his plan can end extreme poverty in the world. All that is needed is for rich countries to give more money to poor countries—in what is known as "the big push." In many ways, the idea is like jump-starting a car. Give a country enough of a jolt of momentum to get going, and soon it will be on the way to a thriving, self-sustaining economy.

With a big push, Sachs argues, ending poverty "is much more likely than it seems," and "success in ending the poverty trap will be much easier than it appears."

For Sachs, the answer is a big plan, based on the United Nations Millennium Development Goals, which are:

- Eradicate extreme hunger and poverty

- Achieve universal primary education

- Promote gender equality and empower women

■ Reduce child mortality

■ Combat HIV/AIDS, malaria, and other diseases

■ Ensure environmental sustainability

■ Develop a global partnership for development

To implement these goals, development experts and leaders from countries around the world have developed a set of 449 interventions—or action steps—to put the plan into motion. The success of the entire plan relies on each of these 449 interventions working together.

How Long Must We Sing This Song?

However, such interventions are unlikely to happen, according to William Easterly, a former World Bank economist who is now a professor at New York University. Easterly says that there are two great tragedies in the world. The first is that so many people suffer in extreme poverty. The second is that so much aid money has already gone to ideas that simply did not work.

Easterly, who first lived in Africa when he was twelve and his father was a visiting biology professor at an African university, begins his book *White Man's Burden* with a speech given by Gordon Brown. At the time Brown, who is now Britain's prime minister, was Chancellor of the Exchequer for the United Kingdom. Articulating the first great tragedy, Brown argued that millions of lives could be saved by distributing medicines that cost less than twelve cents per dose, handing out four-dollar bed nets that can control malaria, and spending three dollars per new mother on maternal health programs in poor countries. Many of those saved would be children.

The second great tragedy, says Easterly, is the failure of Western relief and development efforts over the past fifty years.

This is the tragedy in which the West spent $2.3 trillion on for-
eign aid over the last five decades and still not managed to get
twelve-cent medicines to children to prevent half of all malaria
deaths. The West spent $2.3 trillion and still had not managed to
get four-dollar bed nets to poor families. The West spent $2.3
trillion and still had not managed to get three dollars to each new
mother to prevent five million child deaths.

To Easterly, Sachs's plan sounds like a whole lot more of
what the developed world has been doing for decades—old wine
in new wineskins.

For Easterly, the answer to global poverty is not for Westerners to come up with one great plan to save the world. Instead,
the answer is to help the bottom billion save themselves—to empower what he calls "Searchers"—people committed to solving
one specific problem, in one specific place, and in one specific
time. People who "*can* get twelve-cent medicines to children to
keep them from dying from malaria, *can* get four dollar bed nets
to the poor to prevent malaria, *can* get three dollars to each
mother to prevent child deaths. . . ."

"The world's poor do not have to wait passively for the rich
to save them (and they are not waiting)," says Easterly.

When Love Comes to Town

This kind of approach means seeing poor people not as victims, but as human beings who are capable of finding solutions
to their own problems. It's the approach advocated by veteran
relief workers such as Judy and Dick Anderson.

Following the genocide in Rwanda, the Andersons were sent
to that country by the international charity Tearfund. Both are
veteran relief and development workers, with more than thirty
years experience each. Judy is the daughter of Protestant mis-
sionaries to Congo; Dick is a Vietnam War veteran who, after

seeing the destruction that war caused, devoted his life to doing what he could to help countries and cultures rebuild.

When they arrived in Rwanda in 1994, they decided against bringing in what Dick calls "pre-canned solutions." Instead, they began by meeting with local groups and asking, "What do you need?"—an approach that did not go over well at first.

"This was a time when everyone was feeling guilty and was pouring money into that country," says Judy. During one meeting, a woman asked Judy point-blank, "What does Tearfund want to fund?" She responded by saying, "Tearfund doesn't know what it wants to fund—tell us what you need." At that, the woman became visibly angry. "Don't waste our time," she told Dick and Judy. "Tell us what they want to fund and we will write the proposals." The thought that a Western charity would take time to listen to local ideas before making funding decisions seemed preposterous to her.

A year later, Judy ran into the woman, and she responded differently. They talked about the experience, and the woman told Judy, "Thank you. I didn't realize what you were trying to do."

"We've always come in with our plans and our ideas," Judy says. "People don't expect us to listen. But we don't have all the answers. God does—and He has given wisdom to the most unexpected people in the most unexpected places. But we seldom are ready to listen."

While in Rwanda, Dick heard a BBC interview with a doctor from Goma in the Democratic Republic of Congo on the other side of the border from Rwanda. The doctor, a Congolese surgeon named Dr. Kasereka "Jo" Lusi was the only physician left on staff at a hospital in Goma. He was still doing surgery, while outside the hospital gun battles raged between rebels and government troops. During the interview, gunfire and explosions could be heard in the background. Dick remembers Dr. Lusi telling the BBC interviewer, "I am the only doctor; I couldn't just leave because of the war."

Several times while in Rwanda, the Andersons made plans to cross over into Congo so that they could make contact with Dr. Lusi. The Andersons often act as consultants with relief and development groups, and they thought that they might be able to find some funding to assist Dr. Lusi's work. Each time they arrived at the border, it was closed because of fighting on the other side.

Still, the Andersons kept their eyes out for ways that they could connect with Dr. Lusi. A few years later, Judy was at the Kigali Airport in Nairobi, Kenya, talking with another relief worker. Judy asked the other relief worker if she knew how to get in touch with Dr. Lusi in Goma, Congo. Behind her, a Congolese man asked, "Do you mean me?" Dr. Lusi was standing right behind her. Judy told him that she had access to some funds for programs to assist widows and women hurt by sexual violence during the civil war in Congo. She gave him her e-mail and asked him to be in touch. The next day, she got an e-mail with a list of ideas.

After working with them for several years, Dr. Lusi asked the Andersons if they would help him form a charitable group to support the work. Heal Africa is now run in Goma by Dr. Lusi and his wife, Lyn, while the Andersons raise funds and do logistical support in the United States Much of Heal Africa's work involves training Congolese doctors and providing treatment to rape victims. This can involve surgery to repair fistulas and other injuries, as well as support groups for victims of sexual violence. The group also runs microfinance projects for widows and has trained volunteers to care for AIDS victims.

In Congo and other sub-Saharan African countries, much of the work to be done involves rebuilding communities torn apart by war and ethnic strife or frayed by corrupt governments. "Money does not develop community," Dick Anderson says.

> People develop community. It's not bricks and mortar—it's rebuilding the fabric of a community. It's not us as outsiders who

can do this. It has to be done from the inside. What we have seen in Goma is the determination by people that they are no longer going to sit back and let things go the ways they have been going. They are not going to wait for outsiders to save them. What we can do is to find ways to support people who are already doing heroic things.

Dick goes on to say that "lasting solutions must come from the local population, not from outside."

We have a role to play but I think we have too often over-played our role, and imposed rather than exposed solutions. Creative solutions and adaptations exist everywhere and are so often missed. Each community is unique and while we can share principles learned, the actual program design needs to have local ownership. Too often we exclude the very people we are trying to help . . . the most vulnerable.

Listening to the ideas of local people can lead to unexpected places. In Malawi, the local office of the nonprofit group PSI launched a program to distribute antimalarial bed nets to pregnant women and families with children under five years old— the people most at risk from malaria. The nets have been treated with an insecticide that wards off the mosquitoes that spread malaria. Programs that gave the nets away were ineffective in that part of Malawi—one study found that 40 percent of free nets went unused. Often, nets were either sold off on the black market or used as fishing nets, says Easterly. So PSI began selling the nets for fifty cents each to poor families—with nine cents going to each nurse who sold them. So the nurses have an incentive to keep the nets on hand, and, because they have an investment in the net, people are more likely to use them. PSI also sold nets for $5 to those who could afford to pay more.

The idea of selling bed nets to very poor people seems somehow immoral. But in Malawi, at least, this approach saved lives. Under this program, the number of children and pregnant women sleeping under bed nets jumped dramatically. In 2000, according to a PSI report, only 8 percent of pregnant women and young children slept under bed nets. By 2005, that number had jumped to 55 percent. (A similar program in Mozambique found that selling bed nets did not work as well in that country—another reminder that, when it comes to relief and development, one size does not fit all.)

Voices on the Cell Phone, Voices from Home

In Bangladesh, a Searcher named Iqbal Quadir discovered that one of the best ways to empower poor women in that country was by selling them mobile phones. By doing so, he discovered that money does indeed talk, at least in the developing world. In the early 1990s, Quadir, who had lived and worked in the United States for years, moved back home with the idea of starting a telecommunications company. While working in the United States, he had an epiphany one day when his computer network went down. Without access to the information on his computer, he couldn't do any work. That experience jogged his memory. He recalled how, as a boy, he had been sent to walk ten kilometers to a pharmacy to get medicine for his brother, only to discover that the drug his brother needed was out of stock. He had wasted a whole day because there was no way to talk to the pharmacy ahead of time.

Quadir, whose story is recounted in a book called *You Can Hear Me Now*, realized how much time and productivity was lost in his home country because of the failure to communicate.

Quadir took his idea to Mohammed Yunus, the founder of Grameen Bank and winner of the 2006 Nobel Peace Prize. Years earlier, Yunus had started making microloans to very poor women so they could start small businesses. For example,

Grameen would loan a woman who had no collateral enough money to buy a dairy cow. By selling the cow's milk, the woman could repay the loan and then borrow money for another business venture.

Started in the 1970s, Grameen Bank has lent more than $5 billion to seven million poor women, and has a 98 percent repayment rate. Most of the loans are made to groups of women, who meet on a regular basis and make sure that the loans get repaid. Yunus got the idea for microloans while teaching economics at a local university. Frustrated that the theories he taught seemed to have no relevance to the day-to-day life of poor people, he went out and began talking to local women about what they thought they needed. Most had ideas for starting businesses but could not get credit. Yunus's first loan, for twenty-seven dollars, went to a group of forty-two women.

Why can't a cell phone be a cow? That's the question Quadir asked Yunus. He proposed making small loans to sell mobile phones to "telephone ladies," who would then set up the equivalent of a village pay phone. Launched in 1997, Grameen Phone now partners with more than two hundred thousand telephone ladies, who set up their mobile phones in small shops and rent out minutes. Grameen Bank buys cell-phone minutes and resells them to the telephone ladies at a discounted rate. By 2006, Grameen Phone had annual profits of $200 million, and the telephone ladies were making more than $750 a year, or more than twice the average salary in Bangladesh. In 1997, when Grameen Phone started, there was one cell phone for every five hundred people in Bangladesh. By 2007, that number had dropped to one in eight.

Can a cell phone actually help poor people save themselves? Yes, it can, and several recent studies have shown how.

From 1997 to 2007, a Harvard economist named Robert Jensen monitored sardine markets at fifteen locations in the Indian state of Kerala. Because they had no way to communicate with nearby markets, local fishermen threw away as much as 8 percent of their catch, according to a report on Jensen's work in *The Economist.* "On January 14th 1997, for example, 11 fishermen at Badagara beach ended up throwing away their catches, yet on that day there were 27 buyers at markets within 15km (about nine miles) who would have bought their fish. There were also wide variations in the price of sardines along the coast," *The Economist* reported.

Then cell phones were introduced in the area, and things began to change. By 2007, fishermen were using cell phones to call markets while still at sea in order to find the best price. Better access to markets and better information paid off for everyone. Very few fish were wasted, so that profits for fishermen went up while the price to consumers went down. "Higher profits meant the phones typically paid for themselves within two months," according to *The Economist.* It was a win-win for everyone in the market: fishermen, customers—even the cell-phone provider.

Not only do the telephone ladies and fishermen profit, but, according to a study by Leonard Waverman, an economist at the London Business School, an entire country's economy can be affected by cell phone use. Waverman found that adding ten cell phones per hundred people added about half a percentage point to a country's growth rate. This seemingly small increase in the growth rate is enough to make a country about 5 percent wealthier after ten years, and more than 25 percent wealthier after fifty years. And rather than going into the government's coffers, almost all of the additional profits and wages go to individuals who can use those funds to lift themselves out of extreme poverty.

We Need New Dreams Tonight

None of this means that government funds and foreign aid are not important. They can play a vital role. While Sachs's plan has come under some criticism, it has made people realize that extreme poverty is solvable. Dr. Paul Farmer, founder of Partners in Health and one of the most respected public-health experts, spends half his time teaching at the Harvard School of Public Health and the other half running hospitals and clinics for extremely poor patients in a forgotten corner of Haiti. When *Vanity Fair* magazine ran a special issue on world poverty, Farmer was asked for his opinion of Jeff Sachs's work.

"Just five years ago, people like me who were trying to take care of the destitute sick with diseases like AIDS, we had almost nobody on our side," Farmer said. "We had everyone saying, 'It's not doable, it's too complicated, you need a health infrastructure, it's not sustainable.' Then Jeff got involved in this and said, 'Buck up, stop whining, and start getting work done.'"

And in fairness to Sachs, he agrees that the work of Easterly's Searchers is essential to growth. What Sachs and Easterly disagree on is how to best deliver funding to the Searchers—via a big plan versus piecemeal funding—and on how much the poor country governments should be involved in the process.

So is Bono right? Can Sachs's plan really end extreme poverty? We can't know for sure, but there are reasons to question just how easy the solution will be. Even so, Bono was certainly right when he told the crowd at the National Prayer Breakfast that

> God is in the slums, in the cardboard boxes where the poor play house. God is in the silence of a mother who has infected her child with a virus that will end both their lives. God is in the cries heard under the rubble of war. God is in the debris of wasted opportunity and lives, and God is with us if we are with them. If you remove the yoke from your midst, the pointing of the finger and speaking wickedness, and if you give yourself to the hungry and satisfy the desire of the afflicted, then your light will rise in darkness and your gloom with become like midday and the Lord will continually guide you and satisfy your desire in scorched places.

How can Christian individuals, congregations, and denominations respond to the massive needs of the extreme poor around the world? One way is to support sensible and workable policies in regard to foreign economic development. Easterly and Sachs both agree that much progress can be made through funding for improvements to health care, education, electrification, roads, clean water systems, and sanitation systems.

These sensible and workable solutions include providing money to maintain roads and buildings and water systems, to pay teachers and doctors and nurses, and to buy schoolbooks and uniforms and supplies. Easterly notes that aid agencies have refused to give money for continuing operations and maintenance, viewing these as the responsibilities of the poor country governments. If the government is in disarray because of war or corruption, as is commonly the case, a newly constructed hospital, school, road, or water system can soon fall into disarray. The hospitals lack staff, supplies, and medicine; school buildings don't have teachers, books, or paper; and roads become nearly impassable. Why not reconsider the agencies' refusal to fund operations and maintenance rather than pouring larger amounts of money into new projects that are destined to be inadequately maintained?

Directing more private charitable dollars toward foreign aid for people in extreme poverty can also help. Currently, Americans give about $240 billion to charitable causes. Unfortunately—as Rich Stearns, president of World Vision, notes—less than 3 percent of these donations go to help the poorest people in the world. On a federal level, things are even worse. Less than two tenths of 1 percent of the federal budget is spent on humanitarian assistance. "Our total American commitment right now is not 25 percent of the budget as most Americans seem to think from polls," says Rich Cizik, vice president for governmental affairs of the National Association of Evangelicals. That adds up to about fifteen cents a day per American family. Calling and writing to elected officials, even visiting their offices during an event such as Bread for the World's Lobby Day (in which hundreds of Christians visit Congress to ask officials to do more for poor people), can help as well.

Even more directly, Christians (and everyone else, for that matter) can work on smaller-scale projects to help specific groups of poor people with specific needs that are addressable in measurable ways. Health interventions such as vaccinations, medicines, dietary supplements, and antimalarial bed nets would be highly beneficial and can be done through massive government-level programs or small efforts by groups of interested people. Similarly, providing funds for schools, teachers, and supplies—or actually running a school—is within the scope of even a small- to medium-sized American congregation. Full-scale urban water and sanitation may be too massive for private groups to provide, but rural wells can be constructed, and they can help tremendously.

In any case, the best intervention for churches is not to try to save the world. Instead, it is to find what is working already and serve the people who are making it happen. That's the approach that Willow Creek's leaders adopted when the church first became involved with AIDS relief in Africa. With a congregation of more than twenty thousand, Willow Creek's leaders could have gone to Africa, found a poor community, and imposed their own solutions. Instead, they went to Africa and listened. Then they began supporting groups that were already doing good work. This kind of approach can be replicated in any church of any size.

Lynne Hybels, who heads up the AIDS work at Willow Creek, said in an interview that what strikes her most is seeing the incredible courage and love of churches in Africa. "People suffering from AIDS in Africa are not victims who need to be saved by Westerners," she says. "They are heroes."

"What has impressed me most is the compassion of laypeople in rural African churches, who go into the homes of people with AIDS, bathe them, clean their homes, and take care of their children," she says.

> That level of day in, day out compassion they show is heroic. Whenever we go to Africa or meet with one of our partners, and they thank us for the funds we give, we say, "Are you kidding? What we are doing is so small compared to what you are doing. Thank you for giving us the privilege of being involved in what you do."

6. IS WAL-MART EVIL?

"Each Wal-Mart store should reflect the values of its customers and support the vision they hold for their community."

—SAM WALTON

Two Lines. Two Cities. Two Wal-Mart Stores.

One line was in Uniondale, New York, on Long Island. A crowd had gathered at Grace Cathedral, an evangelical church, preparing for a protest. They would soon march up the street to demonstrate outside the local Wal-Mart as part of a nationwide "Day of Action" on November 21, 2002. The Day of Action, organized by the United Food and Commercial Workers, protested Wal-Mart's treatment of its workers. Demonstrations stretched from Maine to Hawaii.

"'Wal-Mart is going to take your job,' speaker after speaker told the crowd of mostly African-American unionists assembled in Grace Cathedral," reported *The Nation*.

As speakers recited the company's violations of labor rights in China and in the United States alike, loud murmurs of agreement swept through the church, giving it the feel of a revival meeting.

Grace Cathedral's bishop, R. W. Harris, whose congregation includes many Wal-Mart workers, told the crowd: "If Jesus were here today, he'd be at 886 Jerusalem Avenue with you," protesting Wal-Mart.

The second line was in Evergreen Park, Illinois, in January 2006. A new Wal-Mart store was opening in the community, and it was hiring. The store's 325 jobs paid an average of $10.99 per hour. Seventy percent of those jobs were full-time. Wal-Mart says the Evergreen Park store received twenty-five thousand applications. The company's previous high had been eleven thousand applications for a store in Oakland, California. On average, each new Wal-Mart receives between three thousand and four thousand applications.

America has a love-hate relationship with Wal-Mart. For some, it is the epitome of the evils of capitalism. According to its critics, Wal-Mart exploits its workers while grinding suppliers and competitors into the dust. "The truth is that Wal-Mart has let America down by lowering wages, forcing good paying American jobs overseas, and cutting costs with total disregard for the values that have made this nation great," say the organizers of the Wake Up Wal-Mart campaign.

Yet Wal-Mart remains the most popular retailer in the United States. Almost half of consumers shop at Wal-Mart regularly, and job applicants literally line up in the streets for a chance to work there. Some economists argue that Wal-Mart saves U.S. consumers more than $50 billion a year. This means a great deal to Wal-Mart customers such as Steve Rawley from Houston. A small-business owner, Rawley told the *Houston Chronicle* that his diabetes medication, which once cost $44, had been cut to $4 after Wal-Mart began selling a generic version of the drug. "When you have to struggle to get the prescription every month, if you can get any kind of generic for a discounted price, that's a great deal," Rawley said.

Wal-Mart used its clout to cut the price of that drug, according to Loren Steffy, a business columnist for the *Chronicle.* "What other organization has taken such a dramatic step toward lowering health care costs for millions of Americans?" Steffy asked.

> Not insurance companies. Not health care companies. Not the federal government. Wal-Mart, though, offers something unusual: market power. It's known for its ability to extract lower prices from suppliers and pass them on to customers. That alone may make Wal-Mart the single biggest influence in reducing the cost of medicine.

Then she added,

> Here's the crux of the Wal-Mart paradox: We can find fault with a lot of things it does, but we can't deny the benefit. We don't want to shop there, but we inevitably do. The lure of its low prices and convenience makes it seemingly unavoidable. We love to hate Wal-Mart, and we hate that we love it.

The Eight Hundred-Pound Gorilla

The old joke asks, "Where does an eight hundred-pound gorilla sit?" The answer: "Anywhere he wants to!" In many ways, Wal-Mart is the eight hundred-pound gorilla of American business.

Wal-Mart's 2006 revenues of $351 billion put it atop the Fortune 500 list, just ahead of ExxonMobil ($347 billion). If you add up the revenues of Wal-Mart's largest competitors—from Target to the Family Dollar Stores—they still fall $100 billion short of Wal-Mart.

If Wal-Mart were a country (and if revenue and GDP were the same thing), it would be the thirtieth richest in the world.

TABLE 6.1	SELECTED FORTUNE 500 COMPANIES IN 2007			
Rank	Company Name	Revenue in 2006 (billions of dollars)	Profit in 2006 (billions of dollars)	Profit Margin (percent)
Ten Largest Companies:				
1.	Wal-Mart Stores	351	11.2	3.21
2.	ExxonMobil	347	39.5	11.37
3.	General Motors	207	-2.0	-0.95
4.	Chevron Corp.	201	17.1	8.54
5.	ConocoPhillips	172	14.9	9.02
6.	General Electric	168	20.8	12.38
7.	Ford Motor Co.	160	-12.6	-7.88
8.	Citigroup	147	21.5	14.67
9.	Bank of America Corp.	117	21.1	18.06
10.	AIG	113	14.0	12.41
Next Four General Merchandise Companies:				
33.	Target	59	2.8	4.68
38.	Sears Holdings	53	1.5	2.81
76.	Federated Dept. Stores	29	1.0	3.47
116.	J.C. Penney	20	1.2	5.79
Selected Specialty Retailers:				
17.	Home Depot	90.8	5.8	0.58
32.	Costco Wholesale	60.2	1.1	1.83
45.	Lowe's	46.9	3.1	6.62
72.	Best Buy	30.8	1.1	3.70
287.	BJ's Wholesale Club	8.5	0.72	0.84

Wal-Mart employs 1.3 million Americans and another half million people overseas. One out of every 120 American workers works for Wal-Mart. Eighty-eight percent of all Americans live within fifteen miles of a Wal-Mart store, and two-thirds of all retailers are located within five miles of one. A recent survey by The Pew Research Center found that 42 percent of Americans regularly shop at Wal-Mart. Another 42 percent shop there "once in a while." Among Americans with household incomes under $30,000, 53 percent are regular Wal-Mart shoppers.

Eat or Be Eaten

So how did Wal-Mart do it? How did it come to dominate the U.S. retail market? It all started with Sam Walton.

In the 1960s, Walton was a relatively prosperous, small-town businessman. He owned a number of five-and-dime stores in Arkansas, Missouri, and Oklahoma. A born entrepreneur, Walton constantly experimented with ways to cut prices in order to attract more customers. If he found a cheaper price from a wholesaler, he passed the savings on to customers. His stores were also self-service. Rather than dealing with salespeople, customers found what they wanted and brought it to the register themselves. So Walton ran his stores with as few employees as possible, holding labor costs down. His stores earned profits on volume rather than high markups. (Walton was notoriously cheap—even when he became a billionaire, according to *Washington Monthly*, he still got $5 haircuts from a local barber. And he did not leave a tip.)

But Walton saw trouble on the horizon. Retail chains such as K-Mart were using the same discounting techniques and would eventually run small-town stores such as his out of business.

As John Huey put it in a *Time* magazine profile, Walton saw the future and decided to "eat rather than be eaten."

Along with searching far and wide for the best deals from wholesalers, Walton embraced computer technology early on. In 1966, he began looking for a computer programmer to automate the company's business. That led him to a school run by IBM in upstate New York. Walton's goal was "to hire the smartest guy in the class to come down to Bentonville, Arkansas, and computerize his operations," wrote Huey. "He realized that he could not grow at the pace he desired without computerizing merchandise controls."

Walton's obsession with cutting costs is understandable. Despite its success, Wal-Mart, like most other retailers, has a very thin profit margin. In 2006, the company had $351 billion in sales but only $11.2 billion in profits—or just over 3 percent. That $11.2 billion sounds like a lot of money. But compared to other profits at other companies, it's not. ExxonMobil, by contrast, had nearly the same revenue, but it made more than triple the profit, or about $40 billion. Bank of America, with one third the revenue, made double the profit.

Because of their relatively low profits, retail chains such as Wal-Mart have to cut costs wherever possible to stay competitive. This means reducing expenses for warehousing, merchandise processing, and customer checkout, distribution, and transportation.

Because it computerized early, Wal-Mart could operate more efficiently than its competitors. By the late 1970s, according to Emek Basker, an economist at the University of Missouri, Wal-Mart's integrated computer network linked all of its stores and distribution centers to company headquarters. This gave Wal-Mart better control over inventory. In 1990, Wal-Mart likewise integrated its suppliers into a computer network to more closely connect the stores to the suppliers.

Wal-Mart also embraced bar code scanning sooner than the competition. Before bar codes, workers had to slap price stickers on each item that came into the store and ring up each price by hand at the register. With bar codes, both of these tasks could be done cheaper and faster.

Using bar codes and a computer network, Wal-Mart streamlined its order and distribution process. Jon Lehman, a former Wal-Mart store manager, told the PBS program *Frontline* how the company's system works. When he started at Wal-Mart, store employees would place orders, send out invoices, and get new products two weeks later. By the time he left, the process was almost completely automated.

"Let's say you have a cat, and your cat likes tuna-flavored 9 Lives or something. So you go to the counter, and you pick up some tuna 9 Lives. And maybe you pick up some chicken- and some beef-flavored as well, and you take all that to the cashier," Lehman told *Frontline*.

> Well, as soon as that cashier picks up the cans of cat food and scans it, then the cat food is recorded by the computer. The sale's recorded, and then an order is generated. An order is automatically generated that evening at midnight, when the home office pulls that information through their data ports. Then that order goes to the distribution facilities throughout the company, and that distribution facility, the warehouse, fills that order, and it's sitting back on the shelf the next night or the following night.

As Wal-Mart grew, it gained enough clout to negotiate deals directly with suppliers instead of using a middleman. When American companies could no longer meet Wal-Mart's demands, the company began to buy from overseas suppliers. Wal-Mart's size made this outsourcing possible, says Basker and her co-author Pham Hoang Van of Baylor University. Basker and Pham suggest that this is one reason why Wal-Mart abandoned its "Buy American" campaign. Wal-Mart got so big that finding and buying imports were more cost-effective than buying American goods.

Unlike competitors such as Target and K-Mart, Wal-Mart grew by placing new stores near old ones. Once enough stores were in a certain area, Wal-Mart built a distribution center nearby, cutting transportation costs. Plus, having a nearby distribution center allowed stores to have less on-hand inventory at any given time.

Despite its success, Wal-Mart has a reputation for dealing honestly with its suppliers. When *Fast Company* magazine profiled the company in 2003, it reported that "all those interviewed credit Wal-Mart with a fundamental integrity in its dealings that's unusual in the world of consumer goods, retailing, and groceries. Wal-Mart does not cheat suppliers, it keeps its word, it pays its bills briskly."

"They are tough people but very honest; they treat you honestly," Peter Campanella, a former executive at World Kitchen (which sells Corning kitchenware products), told *Fast Company*. "It was a joke to do business with most of their competitors. A fiasco."

Other Wal-Mart suppliers told *Fast Company* that dealing with the retail giant was "like getting into the company version of basic training with an implacable Army drill sergeant. The process may be unpleasant. But there can be some positive results."

"Everyone from the forklift driver on up to me, the CEO, knew we had to deliver [to Wal-Mart] on time," Robin Prever, former CEO of Saratoga Beverage Group, told *Fast Company*.

> The message came through clearly: You have this 30-second delivery window. Either you're there, or you're out. With a customer like that, it changes your organization. For the better. It wakes everybody up. And all our customers benefited. We changed our whole approach to doing business.

Wal-Mart became the largest retailer in the United States by being smarter, tougher, and more innovative than its competitors. It pays its bills on time and doesn't cheat its suppliers. It delivers low prices on products that its customers want. And 84 percent of Americans shop there. So why do so many people hate Wal-Mart?

Always Low Prices, Always Low Wages

Joe Phelps has a few ideas about what's wrong with Wal-Mart. And he's vocal about sharing them. In December 2006,

Phelps—pastor of Highland Baptist Church in Louisville, Kentucky—appeared in a TV commercial asking, "Would Jesus Shop at Wal-Mart?" The answer was "No."

The ad was cosponsored by Wake Up Wal-Mart, an organization that describes itself as "America's Campaign to Change Wal-Mart." In interviews after it ran, Phelps emphasized that Wal-Mart pays low wages to its employees.

"We're grateful for the jobs that they've created but frankly the jobs that they've created don't provide a living wage for a vast majority of their employees, and we think the Bible and the Christian message has something to say about that," Phelps told *CNN Headline News*. And to Fox News' Neil Cavuto he said, "Wal-Mart is creating jobs that on average are below the poverty level, and I don't think that's the kind of company that Jesus would shop at."

How much does Wal-Mart pay? According to the company, its average full-time wage in 2006 was $10.51 per hour. Wal-Mart says that "the majority" of its employees work full-time, meaning between thirty-four and forty hours a week. The average full-time employee earned between $17,867 and $21,020 per year.

Are these poverty wages? It depends. The Census Bureau's 2006 poverty threshold for a family of three is $15,769. For that size family, Wal-Mart's average wages are low but above the poverty line. For larger families, the wages are below the poverty level—if the Wal-Mart employee is the sole breadwinner.

Of course, "average" means that there are workers who are paid less than $10.51. Many at Wal-Mart work part-time and likely earn less per hour than full-time employees. Data obtained from Wal-Mart during litigation showed that 91 percent of Wal-Mart employees earned less than $11 an hour in 2001, as shown in figure 6.1. At that time, the average employee earned $9.70 per hour. (Obviously, Wal-Mart's wage rates have increased between 2001 and 2006.)

FIGURE 6.1   **WAL-MART'S WAGE DISTRIBUTION IN 2001**

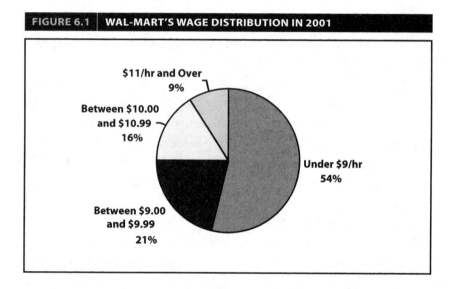

Wake Up Wal-Mart is right on at least one count. Wal-Mart pays lower wages than most other companies. The average wage for all private-sector American workers in 2006 was $18.56. In retail sales, the category Wal-Mart falls into, the average hourly wage was $12.62. Like Wal-Mart's wage distribution, these national averages include many more below-average wages than above-average wages. (However, perhaps none are as skewed as Wal-Mart's wage distribution.) The average full-time Wal-Mart employee makes $2.11—or 16.7 percent less than the national retail average.

Another common criticism of Wal-Mart is that its health insurance plan does not cover all employees. The "Would Jesus Shop at Wal-Mart?" campaign claims that "over 775,000 Wal-Mart workers have no company health care."

Wal-Mart basically confirms this claim. The company reports that 47.4 percent of its more than 1.34 million U.S. employees have health care coverage through Wal-Mart. That leaves over 700,000 workers without company health care.

But Wal-Mart conducted an internal survey in the fall of 2006, which showed that another 35 percent of its employees had health care coverage through a spouse or parent, a prior employer, an individual policy, veterans' or military coverage, or a school or college. Almost 10 percent had no coverage at all. Another 3 percent had coverage through Medicaid or similar state programs. Overall, 76.3 percent of Wal-Mart's workers were eligible for Wal-Mart health coverage, which is based on how long they had worked for the company.

Be Like Costco

The main complaint against Wal-Mart seems to be this: Why can't it be more like Costco?

Costco, the national discount warehouse retailer, currently ranks #32 on the Fortune 500 list. Known as the anti-Wal-Mart, Costco pays the highest wages in the retail sector. Plus, it provides benefits to most of its employees. Recently, *Fortune* magazine dubbed Costco "the only company Wal-Mart fears." The company has become beloved because it seems to offer all of the benefits of Wal-Mart without any of the sins of Wal-Mart.

According to a 2005 *New York Times* article, Costco's average wage was $17 an hour. That's 42 percent higher than Sam's Club, the Wal-Mart-owned store that is Costco's main competitor.

Costco offers a generous retirement plan and low-cost health and dental insurance. Eighty-five percent of its employees have health insurance. Costco CEO Jim Sinegal believes that high pay and good benefits explain Costco's low employee turnover rate and low levels of employee theft.

"Part of it is just sound business thinking. It shouldn't surprise anyone that if you find good people, give them good jobs, and pay them good wages, good things will happen," Sinegal told *Ethix Magazine.*

So if Costco can make money and still pay its employees

well, why can't Wal-Mart? A trip to Wal-Mart and Costco provides some answers.

Would You Like a Hummer with Your Pork Chops?

Travel to the Costco store on Rand Avenue in Lake Zurich, Illinois, and you can pick up a big package of tasty pork chops for $18, some steaks for around $40, a nice leather sofa for around $1,000. Or you could order a Hummer, like the one on display by the store entrance and available through Costco's auto-buying program.

A few driveways over on Rand Road is a Wal-Mart. There you can buy a steno pad for a buck, a copy of the movie *300* for $15.88, or a Godzilla-sized pack of diapers for around $40. There's no Hummer parked in the entranceway—only a fifty-cent, red-convertible kiddy ride featuring the Muppet Fozzie Bear. (A Sam's Club in a neighboring town had a Mercury Mountaineer on display in the store.)

Costco, it turns out, is very different from Wal-Mart. In 2005, Costco had 457 stores worldwide. Wal-Mart has over 3,600. (Sam's Club alone had more stores than Costco.) The average household income of Wal-Mart shoppers is between $40,000 and $45,000. The average Costco shopper's household income is $74,000. What's more, 31 percent of Costco shoppers have a household income over $100,000. (Only 12 percent of American households earn that much.) Costco stores are also concentrated in more affluent areas on the coasts and in major metropolitan areas. And as Sinegal told *Fortune* magazine, Costco stocks only selected items—about 10 percent of what Wal-Mart stocks.

While Wal-Mart serves the general public, Costco focuses on a smaller market. "The business customer is the key member that we service. We also supply a lot of nonprofits like churches, schools, and sports teams. Sixty percent of our business is with business customers," Sinegal told *Ethix*.

Costco, which started in Seattle, paid higher wages from the beginning. Those wages are part of its business plan. In the *Ethix* interview, Sinegal said,

> When we opened our first warehouse in downtown Seattle with forklifts running through stacks of tires and electronics, food and mayonnaise and cranberry juice, people would naturally ask the question, how can they sell things for such low prices? What are these guys doing? We decided that we would take away any objections or questions a customer might have, such as perhaps we could be treating our employees unfairly in order to sell things at low prices.

Wal-Mart, on the other hand, started in the rural south, where wages were and are lower. Two different company histories led to two different approaches to wages and benefits.

There's one other reason why Costco pays more. It hires different sorts of workers than Wal-Mart does. With its industry-leading pay and benefits, Costco *should* be able to attract and retain the best employees in the discount-retailing business. The reality is that some workers are simply more productive than others. If the best retail workers are at Costco, they cannot also be at Wal-Mart.

One person who sees Wal-Mart in this light is Arnold Van Den Berg, a Dutch-born Holocaust survivor who now runs Century Management, an Austin, Texas, investment management service. Van Den Berg's company manages more than $4 billion dollars in financial assets. He sees Wal-Mart stock as a good investment for a number of reasons. Why? It provides jobs for low-skilled workers, and more importantly, Wal-Mart allows workers to gain skills to move up the ladder. As Van Den Berg points out, "Most of Wal-Mart's managers started in entry-level positions and worked their way up. Now for somebody who doesn't have good skills, that's a pretty appealing situation."

In all likelihood, Wal-Mart can't be more like Costco when it comes to wages and benefits. If Wal-Mart were to increase its pay and benefits, it would also have to go after the same higher-skilled workers that Costco thrives on. That would leave the lower-skilled workers with fewer job opportunities.

Cutting Costs or Cutting Corners

With his relentless approach to cost cutting, Sam Walton created the biggest retailer in the world, one beloved by customers for its low prices. But those prices have come at a cost, according to the Wake Up Wal-Mart campaign. In cutting costs, some Wal-Mart stores began to cut corners.

That included breaking child-labor laws and hiring cleaning firms that employed illegal immigrants. Wal-Mart also faces a class-action suit claiming that it discriminated against female employees in pay and promotions.

Has Wal-Mart violated the law? Probably so.

In January 2005, the U.S. Department of Labor reached a settlement with Wal-Mart in a dispute over violations of child-labor laws. The Labor Department found eighty-five violations at Wal-Mart stores in Connecticut, New Hampshire, and Arkansas, where workers under eighteen had been assigned to operate dangerous machinery. In the settlement, Wal-Mart denied any wrongdoing.

In 2001, six women filed a class-action lawsuit against Wal-Mart in a California federal court. The suit alleges company-wide discrimination against women in both pay and promotion. The plaintiffs now represent all women who have worked at Wal-Mart since late 1998—more than 1.5 million women. It is the largest gender-discrimination case ever. Billions of dollars are at stake. The case is still pending. In February 2007, the U.S. Circuit Court of Appeals for the Ninth Circuit concluded that there was sufficient evidence of company-wide discrimination to permit the suit to proceed as a class action. That ruling is not a final finding of fact. But the evidence presented so far raises definite suspicions that Wal-Mart has had a corporate climate that propped up discrimination against female employees.

The discrimination suit is not the only lawsuit Wal-Mart faces. Other employees allege that Wal-Mart managers pressured them to skip breaks and otherwise work while officially "off the clock." In December 2005, a California jury awarded $172 million to workers who, prior to 2001, had been prevented from taking meal breaks in violation of a California law. Other wage-and-hour cases in Oregon, Pennsylvania, and Colorado have also led to jury verdicts against or settlement payments by Wal-Mart. There were still over seventy wage-and-hour suits pending against Wal-Mart in early 2007.

Most companies have lawsuits filed against them, and the biggest companies are often the most attractive targets. Costco, for example, also faces a class-action lawsuit, which claims that a "glass ceiling" keeps women out of store-manager jobs. So, we shouldn't decide that Wal-Mart is evil just because there are lawsuits out there.

But juries have concluded that Wal-Mart violated wage and hour laws, and the Department of Labor found sixteen- and seventeen-year-olds operating hazardous equipment in violation of child-labor laws. A court has found "substantial evidence" of company-wide discrimination against women. Wal-Mart customers have valid concerns that their money is supporting various illegal practices. And Wal-Mart's critics rightly point to illegal practices as a significant problem at Wal-Mart.

Feeding Wal-Mart Is No Picnic

Some suppliers also raise concerns about Wal-Mart. Vlasic, for example, learned that supplying Wal-Mart can be profitable—and perilous. Vlasic makes its money selling cut pickles in jars—dill spears, hamburger chips, and so on. But in the late 1990s, a Wal-Mart buyer got interested in Vlasic's one-gallon jar of whole dill pickles.

Working with Vlasic's sales team, Wal-Mart placed the gallon jars in its stores for $2.97, less than most supermarkets charged for a quart of cut pickles. Wal-Mart shoppers loved the cheap gallons of pickles. Steve Young, a former Vlasic vice president, told *Fast Company* magazine that Wal-Mart "was selling 80 jars a week, on average in every store." According to *Fast Company*, that added up to "240,000 gallons of pickles, just in gallon jars, just at Wal-Mart, every week. Whole fields of cucumbers were heading out the door."

The gallon pickle jar changed Vlasic's business, accounting for 30 percent of the company's sales—and driving profit margins down. Big pickle jars cut into sales of the higher-margin cut pickles. Young said, "We saw consumers who used to buy the spears and the chips in supermarkets buying the Wal-Mart gallons. They'd eat a quarter of a jar and throw the thing away when they got moldy. A family can't eat them fast enough."

When Vlasic went to Wal-Mart to seek a price increase on the gallon jars, Wal-Mart said more than just "no." It threatened to switch suppliers or even stop carrying Vlasic at all. So Vlasic continued selling cheap gallons of whole dills at Wal-Mart for as long as it could. Finally, Wal-Mart relented and allowed Vlasic to offer a half-gallon jar of whole dills for $2.79.

The Vlasic story shows how Wal-Mart pressures its suppliers to cut costs in order to offer "every day low prices." Many suppliers can't manage it, and they fall into financial turmoil trying to satisfy Wal-Mart's requests. Those who succeed, however, benefit from the greater levels of efficiency.

Some companies avoid the Wal-Mart squeeze because they make products that Wal-Mart shoppers will not do without. *Fast Company* reports that this includes "strongly branded" items such as toothpaste, laundry detergent, and sodas. But all of Wal-

Mart's suppliers are faced with a tough choice: Do business the Wal-Mart way or give up on selling your product at the store where 84 percent of America shops at least once in a while. Many of Wal-Mart's suppliers have reacted to the pressure to lower costs by moving production overseas, a topic we'll tackle in chapter 8.

As a retailer, Wal-Mart puts intense pressure on its suppliers to lower costs, and it puts intense pressure on itself to keep its own costs as low as possible. All of this is so that Wal-Mart can fulfill the promise painted above the entrance to its supercenters: "Always low prices."

Always Low Prices!

Many Wal-Mart critics have pushed the company to make small changes in its wage practices. If Wal-Mart could raise prices by 1 percent, they argue, that would enable it to raise wages by an average of $2 per hour.

One percent—a penny on the dollar—seems a small price to pay for better wages at Wal-Mart. But even a small increase could have a monumental effect. That's because Wal-Mart's prices affect more than just its customers' pocketbooks. They also hold down prices across the entire U.S. economy.

Several researchers have concluded that Wal-Mart's prices are between 8 and 27 percent lower than its competitors' prices, depending on the item. Wal-Mart's relentless drive to keep its own prices low doesn't just keep prices low at Wal-Mart. Emek Basker has found that Wal-Mart's entry into a new city reduces competitors' prices by 1 to 3 percent.

These lower prices find their way into the most popular official measure of price inflation in the United States—the Consumer Price Index (CPI). A 2005 study done by the firm Global Insight concluded that Wal-Mart's pricing kept down inflation between 0.1 and 0.2 percentage points a year from 1985 to

2004. (Admittedly, this study was commissioned by Wal-Mart, but it did also find that Wal-Mart had the effect of slowing wage growth across the whole economy by about 0.1 percentage points.) Economists Jerry Hausman of MIT and Ephraim Leibtag of the U.S. Department of Agriculture have concluded that the method for calculating the Consumer Price Index does not adequately take into account Wal-Mart's lower prices. They estimate that by ignoring Wal-Mart's low prices, the CPI overstates total inflation by perhaps 0.5 percentage points or more.

So Wal-Mart lowers prices across the economy in a noticeable way. And lower price levels across the whole economy are basically a pay raise for everyone. A half-a-percentage-point raise may not seem like a lot to one person, but the savings add up when every person in America gets a half-point raise.

Hero or Villain?

Is Wal-Mart evil? Or is it a blessing? The answer seems to be somewhere in between. Wal-Mart keeps prices low in a way that benefits American consumers in measurable ways. But Wal-Mart doesn't pay very well, it squeezes suppliers tightly to cut costs, and it seems to have been cavalier about complying with labor laws.

Would Jesus shop at Wal-Mart? He might. After all, Jesus was poor. Wal-Mart shoppers are disproportionately poor, and they benefit most from Wal-Mart's lower prices. By focusing only on labor practices, Wal-Mart's critics ignore another important part of the picture—the part where Wal-Mart contributes to higher living standards for all poor people by keeping prices down.

That's what Kenneth Stone, a retired Iowa State University professor, found when he was hired by business owners in Kodiak, Alaska, in the 1990s. Wal-Mart was considering opening a store on the island, and Stone was asked to assess the store's potential impact. What he found was that when Wal-Mart comes to town, other businesses suffer. But he also discovered that Wal-Mart helps poor families have a better standard of living. "A lot of low-income people were practically begging the city to let Wal-Mart in," Stone told *The Christian Science Monitor* in 2005. "I believe that the lower prices do allow for a higher standard of living for low-income people."

Wal-Mart could pay its workers more. It could ease up on its suppliers. But it might not be able to do that and still be Wal-Mart.

Only time will tell for sure. But some changes are already underway, at least in terms of obeying the law. In February 2006, CEO Lee Scott sent an internal message to company managers. As reported in *The New York Times* and *Washington Monthly*, the message said: "If you choose to do the wrong thing . . . if you choose to take a shortcut on payroll, if you choose to take a shortcut on a raise for someone, you hurt this company. And it's not unlikely in today's environment that your shortcut is going to end up on the front page of the newspaper."

But that penny-per-dollar price hike and the $2-an-hour pay raise that could go with it? That seems unlikely, especially in the short term.

As T. A. Frank wrote in the *Washington Monthly,*

Wal-Mart is led by people whose lives are devoted to coming up with ways to shave a penny—or a half penny, or a quarter penny—off of a dollar. Wal-Mart's chief spokesman summed up the difficulty in an interview with *The New York Times*. Change might be necessary, he admitted, but "at the same time, we can't change who we are—we can't change what makes Wal-Mart Wal-Mart."

7. HOW DID BEN AND JERRY GET SO RICH?

In the summer of 1978, armed with a few thousand dollars, a used rock-salt-and-ice freezer, a hammer (used for smashing Oreos), and *Ice Cream*, a standard textbook by Wendell S. Arbuckle, Ben Cohen and Jerry Greenfield began selling home-made ice cream out of a renovated 1940s-era gas station in Burlington, Vermont. They were so strapped for cash that they paid for most of the renovations with promises of "free ice cream for life."

For the most part, Ben and Jerry had no idea what they were doing. Ben had once driven a Pied-Piper ice-cream truck, and the two had taken a mail-order course in ice-cream making from Penn State. That was the extent of their ice-cream expertise.

What they lacked in experience, however, they made up for in imagination. Along with chocolate, vanilla, strawberry, and chocolate chip, they sold flavors such as Piña Colada, Banana Rum, and Honey Almond Mist. They made new flavors each day, tossing in new ingredients all the time. Sometimes the results were genius. Oreo Mint, which consisted of smashed cookies in mint ice cream, was a hit. Lemon Peppermint Carob Chip, on the other hand, was not. Neither was Honey Apple Raisin Oreo.

Ben and Jerry's initial scoop shop did better than expected, earning more than $150,000 in the first year. Still, they were barely breaking even. The problem was that they liked to give away too much ice cream. Their small cone sold for only fifty-five cents, tax included, but those cones weren't particularly small. As Fred Lager recounts in *Ben & Jerry's: The Inside Scoop*, the two friends "became resigned to the fact that they were never going to figure out how to control portions in their shop and as a result, they would never make any money."

Looking for a way to add business and control costs, Ben and Jerry started selling their ice cream to local stores. That went so well that their ice cream eventually caught the attention of *Time* magazine. In August 1981, *Time* wrote, "What you must understand at the outset is that Ben & Jerry's in Burlington, Vermont, makes the best ice-cream in the world." The article did go on to mention other contenders for the "best in the world" crown, but for Ben and Jerry's, the article was a marketing dream.

Ben and Jerry's creativity and marketing savvy—inventing flavors such as Chubby Hubby, Chunky Monkey, Wavy Gravy (named after one of the heroes of Woodstock), Cherry Garcia, and one of the first versions of Chocolate Chip Cookie Dough— along with national publicity, soon made their company a household name. By 1985, the company's stock was being publicly traded, following an initial public offering that raised almost $6 million.

A pair of self-described hippies, Ben & Jerry ran their company according to 1960s-style values that they labeled "Caring Capitalism." Neither wore a tie; like their employees, the founders preferred jeans and T-shirts. They paid well—their starting wage was $8 in 1992—and offered benefits and profit-sharing. Ben and Jerry's even had a "Joy Gang" devoted to employee happiness.

Not content to be merely profitable, Ben and Jerry wanted to change the world with their company. They donated profits to charity and political causes, and became evangelists for "Caring Capitalism." *The Economist* labeled them "Raspberry Rebels." Along with their socially conscious values, Ben and Jerry made fair wages part of their business plan. They even put a cap on executive wages—the CEO could make no more than seven times the salary of the lowest paid employee.

By the time Ben and Jerry sold their company to Unilever, an international conglomerate, their ice cream was available in grocery stores and retail ice-cream shops in about a dozen countries. The company sold for $326 million. Since they held much of the company's stock, Ben and Jerry became multimillionaires.

Tiger Woods and Lake Wobegon

Stock options (and stock ownership, such as Ben and Jerry had) help explain why so many chief executive officers (CEOs) make so much money. *Forbes* magazine tracks how much the CEOs at the five hundred largest companies in the United States make each year, and the results are astounding.

These Fortune 500 CEOs are an elite group. In 2006, their median income was $6.7 million. Atop the list was Steve Jobs of Apple, who received an annual salary of only $1.00 but made $647 million through stock options. Eight of the five hundred CEOs received more than $100 million in 2006. Just over a third of them—about 175 in all—received at least $10 million. Almost half of this money came from stock options.

What are stock options, and why do CEOs make so much from them? Stock options are an agreement that, at some future date, the corporation will sell shares of stock at an "option price." If the stock's market price is above the option price when the exercise date rolls around, then the CEO can buy the stock and resell it at a tidy profit.

For example, a CEO might have an option to buy 100,000 shares of stock in five years for $50 each. If the company's stock is trading for $100 per share on the exercise date, then the CEO can buy the stock for $5 million and resell it for $10 million. That's a quick profit of $5 million. But if the market price is below $50 on the exercise date, the option is worthless.

Corporations began to use stock options in the 1980s and 1990s to solve what's known as a "principal-agent problem." The corporation is a principal that hires the CEO as its agent. The corporation is really the shareholders—everyone who owns stock in the company. Their main goal is to increase the long-run value of their stock.

But agents—including CEOs—often have other goals as well. For example, CEOs feel pressure to give in to employee demands, as well as pressure from the media and public. CEOs may also seek certain perks for themselves. These can include everything from expensive art in the executive suite to free memberships in expensive clubs to vacation trips on the company jet. CEOs can meet these other goals by spending company money. This reduces profits and drives down stock prices.

To get around a principal-agent problem, principals have to create reward systems that bring agents' incentives in line with their goals. This is where stock options come in. The company can pay the CEO with options to buy stock several years down the road, with an exercise price above the current market value. To earn anything from the options, the CEO has to increase the value of the company's stock—which is exactly what the shareholders want the CEO to do. In 1980, stock-option profit was only a small part of CEO pay in large corporations. In 2006, almost half of CEO pay came from stock options.

Another piece in the principal-agent puzzle comes from something known as "tournament theory." It explains why CEOs make so much more than the vice presidents right below them on the company ladder—often more than double the vice presidents' pay.

As we saw in chapter 4, a worker's pay is tied to their

productivity. That's true even for managers. But promoting a person from vice president to CEO probably won't make that person more than twice as productive as before.

This is where tournament theory comes in. The idea comes from the world of sports—where tournament prizes draw out maximum effort from all of the athletes involved. In golf and tennis, for example, there is a huge gap in the payoffs between first and second place. In the PGA's 2005 Masters Tournament, Tiger Woods and Chris DiMarco were tied after four days of play. Woods beat DiMarco by one stroke on the first hole of a sudden-death playoff. That one shot earned Woods $1,260,000 for first place. DiMarco received $756,000 for finishing second.

Similarly, in tennis's 2005 U.S. Open, Maria Sharapova won $1,200,000 by defeating Justine Henin-Hardenne, who took home "only" $600,000. The finalists in these events put on great shows because they wanted to win, but also to get the big prize for finishing first.

It may seem strange to think about the corporate rat race as a tournament with a big prize for the winner. But the comparison has some value. In the corporate world, the players in the tournament are all of the vice presidents and other managers who aspire to reach the CEO's office. Corporate tournaments are open to more than just the top two contenders, so the attractiveness of the prize—the fat CEO pay package—motivates a lot more people than the sports prize does. Research on executive pay shows that corporate tournaments work to overcome the principal-agent problem throughout the management hierarchy, and making the tournament work requires a big top prize. This may be a major reason why CEOs get paid so much money.

There is another possibility, though: the Lake Wobegon effect, named after Garrison Keillor's fictional Minnesota town of Lake Wobegon where "all the women are strong, all the men are good-looking, and all the children are above average."

In a roundtable discussion published in the *Harvard Business*

Review, Edgar S. Woolard Jr., former CEO of DuPont, perfectly described the Lake Wobegon effect on CEO pay. "The main reason compensation increases every year is that most boards want *their* CEO to be in the top half of the CEO peer group, because they think it makes the company look strong," he said. "So when Tom, Dick, and Harry receive compensation increases in 2002, I get one too, even if I had a bad year." When boards of directors work hard to keep their CEOs "above average," the average pay rises quickly.

Woolard went on to explain how DuPont solved the Lake Wobegon problem. "We use the pay of the senior vice presidents—the people who actually run the businesses—as a benchmark and then decide how much more the CEO ought to get." In other words, DuPont set up a tournament prize just big enough to get all of the senior vice presidents to work hard.

Rising Ratios

Critics of high CEO pay have focused on an easy-to-understand measure: the ratio of CEO pay to the pay of typical workers. For example, the Institute for Policy Studies and the advocacy group United for a Fair Economy have reported this measurement every year since 1990 for about 350 to 400 large American corporations. In 1990, the average CEO of these companies earned 107 times as much as an average production worker. In 2005, the ratio had grown to 411 after peaking in 2000 at 525.

This ratio reflects a nagging truth: CEO pay in large corporations has grown faster than the pay of most other workers. This growing disparity angers most Americans. A June 2007 Bloomberg/*Los Angeles Times* poll found that more than 80 percent of Americans believe that CEOs are paid too much.

Holly Sklar is a syndicated columnist and coauthor of Let Justice Roll's *A Just Minimum Wage* report discussed in chapter

4. In a June 2007 radio interview, she summed up how many Americans feel: "It's so hypocritical and disgusting that, at the same time they're saying 'lower wages, lower benefits are the way to have a solution here to our economic problems,' you see the CEOs, the people at the top, hoarding more and more."

Jim Wallis, founder of *Sojourners* magazine and author of *God's Politics*, agrees. In a January 2007 press conference on Capitol Hill, he said that the 400-to-1 CEO pay ratio "means the average worker has to work a whole year to make what their boss makes in one day. This is wrong; it's an injustice; it's a theological issue."

This growing disparity has even angered economists. William McDonough, then-president of the Federal Reserve Bank of New York, told a 2002 Washington, D.C., audience that he could "find nothing in economic theory to justify the levels of executive compensation that are widely prevalent today."

Harry Potter and Cherry Garcia

Is high pay only a problem for CEOs? Other highly paid professionals don't receive nearly the criticism that CEOs experience. Since publishing the first of her Harry Potter novels in 1997, author J. K. Rowling has amassed a fortune worth about $1 billion. Ben and Jerry pocketed millions of dollars when they sold their ice-cream company to Unilever in 2000. Even Steve Jobs of Apple was criticized mainly for receiving backdated options and not for his $647 million gain on stock options in 2006.

There is no moral outrage over these massive fortunes. When J. K. Rowling released *Harry Potter and the Deathly Hallows*, she made tens of millions of dollars—while clerks at Barnes & Noble stayed up past midnight to sell the book and likely were paid around $10 an hour. But Jim Wallis didn't worry over Rowling's billion versus the pay of the clerks at Barnes & Noble.

Holly Sklar didn't rail against Ben and Jerry's millions compared to the wages of the high school kids working in scoop shops. So the mere fact that CEOs make a lot more than average workers is not automatically suspicious. Something else must be going on.

Maybe we have a natural tendency to treat creators differently. Maybe it matters that Rowling and Ben and Jerry created the things that made them rich, while Wal-Mart CEO Lee Scott merely manages the empire that Sam Walton created. Such logic underestimates the creativity needed to keep companies alive and thriving.

Also, amid the outrage over CEO excesses, it's easy to overlook the fact that most CEOs don't run Fortune 500 companies or make millions of dollars. According to the Bureau of Labor Statistics, there were about three hundred thousand CEOs in the United States in 2006. Only five hundred—or 0.17 percent—of them could be in the Fortune 500. The average annual earnings of all three hundred thousand CEOs was $144,600. This is one of the best-paying jobs in the United States, granted, about the same as the best-paid physicians. But it is a far cry from the millions of dollars paid to the CEOs of the Fortune 500 companies. And it is only 4.9 times more than the $29,544 earned by the average hourly production worker in 2006.

The Lake Wobegon effect exists in large, publicly traded companies. CEOs in smaller companies are not paid anywhere nearly as well. And this has implications for a Christian response to high CEO pay.

Keep Watch

Can individual Christians do anything about CEO pay? The gap between rich and poor should trouble them. As the Scriptures point out, "The righteous care about justice for the poor, but the wicked have no such concern" (Proverbs 29:7). Amos rails against the "women who oppress the poor and crush the needy," calling them "cows of Bashan on Mount Samaria" (Amos 4:1–2). And Micah asked the leaders of Jacob, "Should you not know justice, you who hate good and love evil; who tear the skin from my people and the flesh from their bones; who eat my people's flesh, strip off their skin and break their bones in pieces; who chop them up like meat for the pan, like flesh for the pot?" (Micah 3:1–3).

One way for Christians to live out these biblical concerns is to keep a watchful eye over companies where their churches have some clout.

Most individual Christians don't own enough stock for big companies to pay attention to them. But "institutional investors" do have a lot of clout with big companies. These are the banks, pension funds, mutual funds, insurance companies, and other large businesses that own trillions of dollars worth of stock. Unlike most people, institutional investors own enough stock to make a difference in shareholder votes. As Berkshire Hathaway CEO Warren Buffett told *Fortune* magazine, "The only cure for better corporate governance is if the small number of very large institutional investors start acting like true owners and pressure managers and boards to do the same."

Many Christian organizations are institutional investors—via pension funds and church endowments, for example. Guide-Stone Financial Resources of the Southern Baptist Convention has over $10 billion in assets. Thrivent Financial for Lutherans manages $70 billion in assets. Other denominations, religious colleges, and organizations such as the Knights of Columbus—all of these manage large investment funds. Together, these religious organizations could wield the market clout of Buffett's "very large institutional investors." They could push for reasonable approaches to CEO pay in the large companies whose stocks they own.

Economists developed tournament theory to explain why large corporation CEOs make so much money. But these CEOs make too much for tournament theory to explain. Stock-option programs were started to solve a principal-agent problem, but they have quickly grown out of control.

Christians can do more than condemn such practices. They can change them by getting their church's institutions to act like owners. And if church-based colleges, denominations, pension funds, and other institutions begin speaking the words of Scripture, CEOs and corporate boards will have to listen.

YOU WERE ALIENS

God doesn't play favorites with nations. His covenant with Abraham promised that all nations would be blessed through Abraham's descendants (Genesis 18:18; 22:18; 26:4). He commanded Jonah to preach to Nineveh. Jonah didn't want to go because he feared God would have mercy on the city. God made Jonah go anyway, and used him to turn the Ninevites from their evil ways (Jonah 1:2; 3:2, 10; 4:2).

In God's promised world, nations come together as one (Zechariah 2:11; Revelation 21:24–26). Jesus came to *"proclaim justice to the nations"* (Matthew 12:18). His disciples were to be *"witnesses in Jerusalem, and in all Judea and Samaria, and to the ends of the earth"* (Acts 1:8).

The Bible is even clearer when it comes to immigrants. After fleeing to Midian, Moses said of himself, *"I have been a stranger in a strange land"* (Exodus 2:22, KJV). The Law given to Moses commands, *"Do not oppress an alien; you yourselves know how it feels to be aliens, because you were aliens in Egypt"* (Exodus 23:9). Psalm 146:9 declares that *"the Lord watches over the alien, and sustains the fatherless and the widow, but he frustrates the ways of the wicked."* Leviticus 19:33–34 elaborates: *"When an alien lives with you in your land, do not mistreat him. The alien living with you must be treated as one of your native-born. Love him as yourself, for you were aliens in Egypt. I am the Lord your God."*

In His very first sermon, Jesus promised that the kingdom of God included those outside Israel—such as the widow of Zarephath and Naaman the Syrian (Luke 4:24–27). In John 4, Jesus assured the Samaritan woman at the well that she could receive the living water of eternal life. And Jesus' example of a loving neighbor was the Good Samaritan of Luke 10:25–37.

The Bible emphasizes that Christians must care for foreigners and immigrants. How can these biblical standards be applied to trade and immigration policy? We take up this question in the next two chapters.

8. DOES GLOBALIZATION EXPLOIT THE POOR?

"If a foreign country can supply us with a commodity cheaper than we ourselves can make it, better buy it of them with some part of the produce of our own industry employed in a way in which we have some advantage."

—ADAM SMITH, *THE WEALTH OF NATIONS*, BOOK IV, CHAPTER II

Julie Clawson needed a new bra.

Most of the time, Clawson, a Chicago-area, church-planting pastor, would have gone to Victoria's Secret, plunked down some cash, and headed home with a new bra. But she had been doing some reading about globalization, and her conscience now wondered about where her money was going and what was being done with it. So she decided to try an experiment. Julie Clawson decided to find a "justice bra"—one that could do no wrong.

This bra had to meet some high standards. "The bra had to be made from an organically grown material. No synthetics made from petroleum, no pesticides that harm the environment and the farmers, and no unsustainable practices," she wrote on the *God's Politics* blog. The bra must be made without toxic dyes, and it had to be "fairly made." From the farmers who grew the fibers, to the weavers who spun the fabric, to the tailors who assembled it, each person (adults, not children) along the way had to have been paid a living wage (usually much more than minimum wage), not been coerced to work, and treated humanely.

"Whoever made my bra needs to be able to make a living doing so," Clawson wrote. "And not a degrading, oppressive living either, but one that treats them as a real person."

Did such a bra exist? After searching for a couple of weeks, Clawson found one. An online retailer, based on Vancouver Island off the western coast of Canada, had a U.S.-made organic-cotton bra that met her "justice bra" standards at a price of about $30—not much more than she would have spent at the mall, Clawson wrote.

It's not just underwear that raises justice issues. Most of our clothes—and many other products we use each day—are made overseas. For example, the documentary *China Blue* shows what life is like for Chinese workers who make the blue jeans that Americans wear. "They live crowded together in cement factory dormitories where water has to be carried upstairs in buckets," says the film's PBS Web site. "Their meals and rent are deducted from their wages, which amount to less than a dollar a day."

China Blue tells the story of seventeen-year-old Jasmine, who moved from a rural village to the city of Shanxi in the booming Guangdong province:

> She shares a room with 12 other girls and labors every day from 8 a.m. until 2 a.m., seven days a week, removing lint and snipping the loose threads from the seams of denim jeans. Jasmine's initial excitement to be able to help her family with her wages quickly dissipates as she is overwhelmed by the long work hours and the delays in pay. The strong friendships she forms with her co-workers and memories of home are her only solace.

"Globalization" means a lot of different things, and we can't possibly talk about all of them in a single chapter. We can, however, examine some global issues that matter to a lot of people— namely, "outsourcing," overseas labor standards, and trade policy. In chapter 9, we'll explore immigration to the U.S.

T-Shirts and Turtles

On a winter day in 1999, Pietra Rivoli, a finance and international business professor at Georgetown University, watched a student protest. A group of one hundred students gathered in the center of campus, shouting out slogans. "Corporations, globalization, the International Monetary Fund (IMF), and the World Trade Organization (WTO) were the bad guys, ruthlessly crushing the dignity and livelihood of workers around the world," Rivoli later recalled.

Then a young woman stepped to the microphone. As Rivoli listened in, the student asked, "Who made your T-shirt?" She went on:

> Was it a child in Vietnam, chained to a sewing machine without food or water? Or a young girl from India earning 18 cents per hour and allowed to visit the bathroom only twice per day? Did you know that she lives 12 to a room? That she shares her bed and has only gruel to eat? That she is forced to work 90 hours each week, without overtime pay? Did you know that she has no right to speak out, no right to unionize? That she lives not only in poverty, but also in filth and sickness, all in the name of Nike's profits?

Rivoli realized that she didn't know the answer to those questions. And she doubted the student did either. So she decided to find out. While on vacation in Florida, she bought a $6 T-shirt with a picture of a parrot on the front of it, and over the next five years traced the shirt's history.

As she describes in her book *The Travels of a T-Shirt in the Global Economy,* Rivoli began by reading the label: "Made in China." She tracked the shirt back to Sherry Manufacturing, a Miami silk-screener who printed the design onto the shirt. They connected her with Xu Zhao Min of Shanghai Knitwear, which sold the shirt to Sherry. When Xu, who goes by the nickname "Patrick," was next in the States, Rivoli invited him to Georgetown.

Sitting in her office, Rivoli asked Patrick if she could visit him in China and see where the shirts were sewn, the fabric was knit, and the yarn was spun. Patrick said he could show her all of these places. Rivoli also knew that China was one of the world's biggest cotton producers. So she asked, "Could I go to the farm and see how the cotton is produced?"

Patrick's response surprised her. "Well, that might be difficult," he said. "I think the cotton is grown very far from Shanghai. Probably in Teksa." Rivoli pulled out a globe and turned it to China. She asked where exactly "Teksa" was. Patrick laughed, turned the globe back around, and pointed. "Here, I think it is grown here," Patrick said.

"Patrick was pointing at Texas," she wrote.

Rivoli's story reminds us that trade is a two-way street. And it's not just cotton that makes its way from Texas to China. Reuters recently reported that Texas turtle hunters have also embraced globalization. An average of 92,000 turtles a year are captured in Texas for export. Between 2002 and 2005, 267,000 wild turtles were shipped from Texas to Hong Kong. Some end up as exotic house pets, but most get eaten. In Asia, turtle meat is a delicacy.

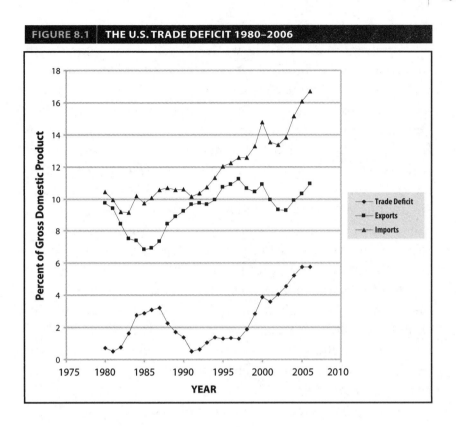

FIGURE 8.1 | THE U.S. TRADE DEFICIT 1980–2006

Sending Jobs Overseas

The U.S. imports more goods and services than it exports (see figure 8.1). The U.S.-trade deficit in goods and services was over $750 billion in 2006, or 5.8 percent of the GDP. The deficit has generally gone up as a percentage of the GDP since 1991. Most of the increase is because of more imports. Exports have fluctuated around 10 percent of the GDP, but imports have grown from about 10 percent of the GDP in 1990 to more than 16 percent in 2006.

Few economists are worried about the growth in international trade. One of the things on which almost all economists agree is that free trade makes both trading countries richer. This understanding dates all the way back to Adam Smith. "If a foreign country can supply us with a commodity cheaper than we ourselves can make it," he wrote, "better buy it of them with some part of the produce of our own industry employed in a way in which we have some advantage."

To understand why this works, think about your own life. Few of us produce everything we need. We don't grow our own food, make our own clothes (much less grow the cotton from which to make it), or build our own houses. Rather, we specialize and trade. We sell our labor services in a labor market, and we use that money to buy the food, clothing, houses, cars, and other goods and services that we need. Countries do the same thing. Sometimes countries trade because they can't produce a certain good. For example, Japan needs crude oil but has no major oil deposits, so it has to trade with other countries for the oil it needs. Most of the time, however, countries specialize in things that they're good at. For example, Brazilians grow bananas, while Americans raise apples. Then, we trade with each other, depending on how much Americans want bananas and Brazilians want apples.

We both have more apples *and* more bananas this way. Brazil is just a better place to grow bananas, and the U.S. is a better place to grow apples. With each country specializing and trading, Americans and Brazilians can all have more apples and bananas.

This idea carries over to every other form of trade. Natural resources help determine each country's specialties. But other factors are also important. Human capital matters. And so does physical capital such as factories and equipment. In general, countries with the lowest levels of human and physical capital produce more basic goods, especially agricultural products. And as countries develop their human and physical capital levels, they move up a "ladder of comparative advantage," as economist Jagdish Bhagwati, author of *In Defense of Globalization*, put it. What a country can best specialize in *changes* as the country becomes richer. The general trend is to specialize in making more skill- and capital-intensive goods as a country gets richer. These ladders of comparative advantage are crucial to seeing why American jobs are not merely being "shipped overseas" or "outsourced." Such terms are loaded with rhetorical power. But all they really mean is that Americans are trading with people in other countries.

In our apples and bananas example, trading didn't mean Americans had nothing to do. If Brazilians grow bananas, that frees up more Americans to grow apples. Similarly, when Japan started making so many consumer electronics, American human and physical capital was freed up to make other things, such as computer microprocessors and high-end financial services. These "other things" that Americans did made more money for Americans.

Specialization even happens within the stages of making a product. Getting a product in a consumer's hands takes several steps: establishing the company brand, developing the product idea, designing the product, manufacturing it, and finally shipping and distributing it. As James Fallows described in *The Atlantic Monthly*, China's role in this product cycle "is in the middle stages—manufacturing, plus some component supply and engineering design—but America's is at the two ends, and those are where the money is." It's not the "good jobs" that are being "outsourced." It's the ones that add the smallest value to the product.

Today, China and South Korea are challenging Japan's spot on the consumer-electronics rung, and Japan is moving up the ladder of comparative advantage. The United States is near the top of the ladder, which is why it is so rich. Even Chinese textile makers are moving up the ladder. Patrick Xu told Rivoli that his Shanghai firm was already being priced out of the market for white T-shirts by lower-wage countries and other parts of China. Consequently, he was "trying to move up the value chain into fancier goods such as sweaters."

Not Everyone Wins

Free and open trade makes nations better off, but there are individual losers among the winning nations. Even Bhagwati, a staunch free trader, admits this. "It is not sufficient that, by and large, globalization advances both economic and social agendas," he wrote. "Everything does not necessarily improve every time!"

Ask American textile workers if they are better off because of textile imports, and they will say no. Yet the price of clothing in the United States has gone up by only 20 percent since 1983. In fact, clothing prices have *fallen* by about 10 percent since 1997, according to the Bureau of Labor Statistics. Most Americans are much better off because of this, even as the textile workers have lost their jobs.

Blocking imports of inexpensive clothing is not the best way to help textile workers. Job retraining programs could help. Industrial redevelopment plans at the local level could help. If a textile job can be replaced by an auto-manufacturing job—such as the BMW plant in Spartanburg, South Carolina—then American workers can be better off. It won't be easy or cheap to help those harmed by more international trade. But the gains from trade for the many are enough to offset the losses to the few. The key is making sure we really do help the few. And as discussed in more detail in chapter 3, Christian groups can help with human-capital programs that seek to pull the few up the ladder of comparative advantage along with the rest of the country.

Dickens Déjà Vu?

In Charles Dickens' *Oliver Twist*, nine-year-old Oliver lands in an orphanage, where meals are a bare portion of gruel. "The bowls never wanted washing," Dickens wrote. "The boys polished them with their spoons till they shone again." Still hungry, the boys sucked on their fingers "most assiduously, with the view of catching up any stray splashes of gruel."

One day, the boys decide to ask for more. The lot falls to Oliver to do the asking. In a famous scene, Oliver finishes his bowl of gruel and returns to the master of the orphanage in the front of the room. "Please, sir, I want some more," he says.

The master responds in the only way that he can imagine, smacking Oliver in the head with the ladle and hauling him before the orphanage's board for discipline. Oliver is immediately locked up alone in a dark cell, while the board offers to give away both Oliver and £5 to anyone who'll take the boy.

In *David Copperfield*, Dickens describes the factory workshop where young David first works. "Murdstone and Grinby's warehouse was at the waterside." It was "literally overrun with rats. Its panelled rooms, discoloured with the dirt and smoke of a hundred years, I dare say; its decaying floors and staircase; the squeaking and scuffling of the old grey rats down in the cellars; and the dirt and rottenness of the place" were all things that stayed in David's memory.

It turns out that Murdstone and Grinby's was engaged in international trade, supplying "wines and spirits to certain packet ships" headed for the East and West Indies. Both men and boys examined used bottles for defects and then washed them for reuse. In Dickens' day, then, sweatshops created by globalization already existed.

Many people are concerned that today's sweatshops are just as "Dickensian" as Oliver's orphanage or Murdstone and Grinby's. Stories abound of unsafe working conditions, bad food and too little of it, unsafe housing, child labor, low pay, and near-slavery.

One organization that tracks sweatshops around the world is Sweatshop Watch. They define a sweatshop as

a workplace that violates the law and where workers are subject to: extreme exploitation, including the absence of a living wage or long work hours; poor working conditions, such as health and safety hazards; arbitrary discipline, such as verbal or physical abuse; or fear and intimidation when they speak out, organize, or attempt to form a union.

Some sweatshops use child labor, says Sweatshop Watch. According to the group's Web site,

> Many child laborers are in exploitative conditions with low wages, long working hours, no medical or welfare facilities, no proper meals or accommodations, no permanent employment status, exposed to dangerous working environments with few educational opportunities. Some children are working under bonded and slave-like conditions, harmful to physical, emotional growth and development.

The blue-jean factory shown in *China Blue* is actually mild compared to horror stories such as this.

Rivoli also talks at length about the working conditions in the Chinese textile industry. Throughout the history of the mechanized cotton-clothing industry, she wrote, the key input needed was a docile labor force willing to do dull, repetitive tasks over long hours with few breaks. Today, that describes the workers in China's textile mills. What makes docile workers? In every country's textile industry across time, docility comes from "a lack of alternatives, lack of experience, and limited horizons"—the same lack of choices discussed in chapter 3.

What Would You Prefer?

Yet to these Chinese textile workers, life in the mills is much better than life back on their farms and in their villages. Liang Ying described her life on the family rubber farm to sociologist Ching Kwan Lee: "It is really hard work. Every morning, from 4 am to 7 am you have to cut through the bark of 400 rubber trees in total darkness. It has to be done before daybreak, otherwise the sunshine will evaporate the rubber juice. If you were me, what would you prefer, the factory or the farm?"

Nicholas Kristof and Sheryl WuDunn are reporters who headed off to China to expose the evils of the sweatshops. They were surprised at what they found. In a *New York Times Magazine* article titled "Two Cheers for Sweatshops," they described their 1987 interviews of young women in a purse-making sweatshop in southern China. They worked twelve hours a day, seven days a week, with a week or two off to go back home at Chinese New Year. The women "all seemed to regard it as a plus that the factory allowed them to work long hours."

"It's actually pretty annoying how hard they want to work," the factory manager told Kristof and WuDunn. "It means we have to worry about security and have a supervisor around almost constantly."

In a 2004 *New York Times* column, Kristof told about Nhep Chanda, a seventeen-year-old Cambodian girl who sifts through the city dump to make a living. She "averages 75 cents a day for her efforts. For her, the idea of being exploited in a garment factory—working only six days a week, and inside instead of in the broiling sun, for up to $2 a day—is a dream."

American sensibilities see sweatshops as inhumane places that exploit young women and girls. Kristof and WuDunn admit that this is true. Workers *do* live in firetrap dorms. Children *are* exposed to dangerous chemicals. Some managers *do* "deny bathroom breaks, demand sexual favors, force people to work double shifts or dismiss anyone who tries to organize a union." But sweatshops have also been the engine of growth in China and other East Asian countries.

In table 5.1, we saw that extreme poverty (living on less than $1 a day) fell in East Asia by more than five hundred million people between 1981 and 2001. Plus, the percentage of East

Asians living in extreme poverty fell from 57.7 percent to 14.9 percent. If we look at the statistics for the number of East Asians who earn less than $2 a day, the numbers are still impressive: Three hundred million fewer people live on less than $2 per day in East Asia, and the portion of East Asians living on less than $2 a day has fallen from 84.8 percent in 1981 to 47.4 percent in 2001.

Smaller gains have occurred in South Asia—including India—mainly because South Asian countries were slower to embrace international trade as a growth strategy. And in the rest of the developing world, poverty has been about the same or even gone up a little because governments have rejected growth strategies based on the export trade.

Bhagwati points to studies showing that jobs in poor-country factories run by multinational corporations pay much better than most other jobs in those countries. Generally, such workers earn up to 10 percent more than comparable jobs in their countries. Some multinationals pay as much as 40 to 100 percent higher. But this pay premium doesn't carry over to the locally owned poor-country subcontractors of multinational firms— they pay the same as all of the other poor-country employers.

The sweatshops pay better than village life, and this has led to less poverty—and better working conditions. Kristof and WuDunn report that wages in Dongguan, China, have risen from $50 a month in 1987 to $250 a month today.

> Factory conditions have improved as businesses have scrambled to attract and keep the best laborers. A private housing market has emerged, and video arcades and computer schools have opened to cater to workers with rising incomes. A hint of a middle class has appeared—as has China's closest thing to a Western-style independent newspaper, *Southern Weekend*.

Less Sweat, More Shop

Some Chinese factories are even getting a lot less sweaty. Andy Mukherjee of Bloomberg.com tells about a massive Chinese factory complex—its two hundred thousand workers outnumber the populations of many U.S. cities—where Apple's iPods are made. Dorms are air-conditioned and have TV rooms, snooker tables, and public telephones. The campus has "soccer fields, a swimming pool, supermarkets, Internet cafes, banks, 13 restaurants and a hospital." The factory appears to comply with Chinese labor laws and doesn't use child labor. All the employees have medical coverage.

The iPod factory is hardly the norm, but it shows what can happen as China's export goods get more valuable and as Chinese workers become more accustomed to their modest but growing wealth.

Back in the apparel trade, Rivoli says that sweatshop jobs help the workers develop a new set of choices. Schooling, independence, release from undesirable arranged marriages, and more all become possible in the workers' few off hours. Such things make these women less docile and thus less suited to their sweatshop jobs. But the women also become "better workers for the expanding industries requiring initiative, decision making, [and] teamwork" that move in as the textile industry moves on to its next dominant country.

Rivoli does not simply ignore poor working conditions, either. In fact, she describes how today's sweatshop jobs in China feature noticeably better working conditions than the past sweatshops of England, the United States, and East Asia. She attributes the improvement over time to the efforts of activists, labor unions, governments, religious leaders, and—most importantly—the workers themselves.

Rivoli hints at a solution for Christians who want to improve substandard working conditions around the globe. Don't try to eliminate the jobs through boycotts and similar tactics. Kristof and WuDunn say that "Asian workers would be aghast at the idea of American consumers boycotting certain toys or clothing in protest." Instead, pressure the employers by shining a light into their practices and making them publicly known. Help the workers learn how to stand up for themselves to get better working conditions. Use the justness of your cause as your best weapon.

Rivoli notes that Georgetown University and many other colleges have improved conditions for workers in China by being willing to pay for better conditions—and by hard bargaining. "We only do business with companies that will disclose their factory locations," she said in an online interview.

> We require all of our companies to have codes of conduct and monitoring systems largely designed to address labor issues. And there are organizations that serve the university community like The Fair Labor Association and The Workers Rights Consortium that did not exist 10 years ago. Both of these are especially important because they really do the legwork of monitoring factory conditions for us. There has been an enormous change.

In that same interview, Rivoli noted that as Chinese factory workers have gotten more skilled, they have gained clout. "What is happening in China now is that the factory workers are holding a lot of power, because there are extreme labor shortages," she said.

> The factories producing textiles cannot find the workers they need to keep producing. The power has shifted. Rather than having millions of people begging for a job and being exploited, you have instead thousands of factories begging for workers. I think that is a sign of progress. China has come a long way. I think it's quite dangerous to make judgments about workers in

China, without talking to workers in China because they have much different things to say than those of us who haven't been in their position.

Bhagwati agrees that public pressure is better than trade sanctions for cleaning up developing-country labor practices. He admits that many people think formal sanctions—such as boycotts and bans and tariffs—will work better at improving overseas wages and working conditions than mere moral persuasion. "I think this is the same as saying that the Pope has no troops. Surely one does not need the rack to spread Christianity," he writes. "Indeed, we must remember that God gave us not just teeth but also a tongue. And a good tongue-lashing on a moral cause is more likely to work today than a bite. Recall that, with NGOs and CNN, we have the possibility now of using shame and embarrassment to great advantage."

Toxic Elmo

Over the span of a few months in 2007, the American media reported on a host of dangerous products from China. Among the millions of recalled products were poisoned pet foods, tires with separating treads, and Fisher Price toys featuring characters such as Big Bird and Elmo, Dora and Diego, that were covered in toxic paint. The wave of recalls raised a furor among Americans. Are goods made in China safe?

Most experts agreed that the dangerous products were only a tiny part of all imports from China. But the perception among U.S. consumers was that Chinese goods couldn't be trusted. This reminded *New York Times* reporter Joseph Kahn of similar problems in another country. "Phony fertilizer destroys crops. Stores' shelves are filled with deodorized rotten eggs, and chemical glucose is passed off as honey. Exports slump when European regulators find dangerous bacteria in packaged meat." Where did all this happen? Right here in the U.S.A.—about one hundred years ago.

The problems Kahn described led to the creation of the Food and Drug Administration in 1906. And the real question raised by the recent rash of highly publicized recalls of Chinese imports is—as the *Times* headline phrased it—"Can China reform itself?" The problem in the United States in 1900 was a lack of regulations, something that was slowly fixed. (Kahn says it took until 1961 for the FDA to get full control over the drug supply.) In China, however, the problem is too many regulators and no clear authority.

According to the *Times*, "As many as 17 bureaucracies have overlapping responsibilities in just the food and drug sphere, and they jealously guard their power." With no clear duties and too many regulators, there is no Chinese government agency to hold responsible. So dangerous products can fall through the cracks— sometimes with the help of bribes paid to the bureaucrats.

It's hard to imagine that the Chinese government will endanger its lucrative U.S.-export trade. Improved regulation is in China's own interest, and there are signs that China may be changing. Consider Zheng Xiaoyu, former head of China's State Food and Drug Administration. He was convicted in May 2007 of taking millions of dollars in bribes in exchange for approving defective foods and medicines—including drugs that killed one hundred Panamanians. After Zheng lost his appeal, the Chinese government executed him in July 2007.

Perhaps the Chinese government is beginning to reform its regulatory system. Even so, American importers and consumers are wise to keep on the lookout for potentially dangerous products, whether made in China or anywhere else.

Protecting Americans and Hurting Poor Countries

Free trade makes the trading countries better off. So it's not a surprise that rich countries have been pushing for decades for more and more free trade. Even though much progress has been made at reducing barriers to trade, some still remain. And they are having an impact on people in poor countries.

One example is the system of subsidies and price supports for American cotton. Another is the maze of quotas and other import restrictions on T-shirts coming back into the U.S. agricultural subsidies cut the prices poor-country farmers can get for their crops in global markets. And the quotas directly limit access of poor-country textile manufacturers to the U.S. market. All of which favors the relatively well-off (and higher cost) American farmers and textile workers at the expense of people living in extreme poverty around the world.

While it is easy to criticize American government protectionism, poor-country governments are far worse. Bhagwati reports that average import taxes were much higher in poor countries than in rich ones. Poor countries certainly should do more to reduce their own trade barriers, but high U.S. and European Union taxes on certain imports compound the problems of the world's poorest people.

Justice Isn't Free

There are limits on how much we'll pay for "justice," even for well-meaning people. In her search for a "justice bra," Julie Clawson had found a $100 one made in the United Kingdom, but she balked at paying such a high price. "I knew this endeavor would require more funds than the typical sale bin at the mall, but I had my limits. There has to be a balance between saving a buck at the expense of a worker in a third world nation and throwing one's money away on luxury items."

And it's not at all clear that Clawson really achieved the greatest justice by buying the justice bra. It was made in the United States and sold by a Canadian retailer. There is no indication that a single poor person was helped in any impoverished country. At best, Clawson could hope for long-term effects—if enough people think like her, then maybe working conditions around the globe could improve more quickly as demand for unjust bras wanes. At worst, buying an American-made bra from a Canadian company made some poor sweatshop worker a little worse off.

Is Clawson's willingness to pay $30 for underwear typical of most Americans? The Wal-Mart store in Lake Zurich, Illinois, mentioned in chapter 6, has a wide selection of bras ranging from $8 to $15. Undoubtedly, these fail Clawson's justice criteria. But they were probably made by poor-country workers, doing jobs they prefer to their other choices. And the low price allows low-income Americans to stretch their hard-earned dollars more.

So which bra does more justice—the $30 one Clawson bought over the Internet or the $8 one at Wal-Mart?

9. ARE IMMIGRANTS TAKING ALL OF OUR JOBS?

Give me your tired, your poor,
Your huddled masses yearning to breathe free,
The wretched refuse of your teeming shore.
Send these, the homeless, tempest-tost to me,
I lift my lamp beside the golden door!

—EMMA LAZARUS, "THE NEW COLOSSUS," INSCRIBED ON THE
BASE OF THE STATUE OF LIBERTY

Inez and Antonio Valenzuela sell tacos. According to *Business Week*, the young couple started with only a small sidewalk stand. Five years later, they were operating out of a $70,000 trailer pulled by an $11,000 used van. They're open eight hours a day, six days a week. They earn more than the U.S.-average-household income. They have checking and savings accounts. They pay income taxes. They dream of someday expanding their business by buying additional trailers.

The Valenzuelas are also in the United States illegally.

Pradip Kothari was born in the state of Gujarat on the northwestern coast of India. *Washington Post* reporter S. Mitra Kalita tells his story in her book *Suburban Sahibs*. Pradip's parents were professionals and active members of India's dominant Congress Party. He graduated from Gujarat's premier university, though he spent more time organizing rallies and advocating causes than studying. In 1972, Pradip moved to the United States as a legal immigrant, at the age of twenty-two. He visited India in 1976 for an arranged marriage to his wife, Nandini. Since the 1980s, Pradip has owned a travel agency on Oak Tree Road in Iselin,

New Jersey, the main business district for central New Jersey's large Indian population.

Pradip is a leader in the local Indian community. After a bout of vandalism targeted Indian businesses in the 1980s, he formed a merchants association on Oak Tree Road. He organized an Indian cultural society that sponsors a major religious festival each year. He put on fund-raisers in the Indian community for candidates for local and state offices. Pradip even ran unsuccessfully for county office.

Nandini Pradip is a medical records supervisor whose work takes her to several different hospitals. Yet at the many events that Pradip organizes, other Indians see Nandini only as Pradip's wife and cohost. Festival fatigue has set in, but Nandini prefers it to the alternative—being a housewife in India, "sitting home all day, watching the kids, supervising cooks and maids and gardeners," according to *Suburban Sahibs*.

And then there are the four unnamed Mexicans whom *National Geographic Adventure* photojournalist John Annerino accompanied across the border between Mexico and Arizona. The men walked through the Sonoran Desert from about 4:00 p.m. until midnight, rested until 4:30 a.m., and set off again. An accomplished desert distance runner, Annerino said,

> If you're trained and acclimated to the heat, you really don't notice it until you become dehydrated. Your muscles become cramped from lactic acid and from the number of hours you're standing upright. You get dizzy, feel nauseous. You can't hold down water. Mine lasted for about 40 miles and then I was out. We just made it because it was starting to cool, and the goal was in sight—in this case Interstate 8.

The five men reached Interstate 8 at about 8:00 p.m. after walking all day, following various landmarks on a route that has been passed along from one generation to the next. Annerino said that crossing the border without being caught is easy if you know what you're doing. What did he learn from the trip? "The extraordinary lengths that human beings will go to make a better life for themselves," he said.

The United States is a land of immigrants. Waves of immigrants arrived from various parts of Europe during the open-borders era of the nineteenth and early twentieth centuries. In 1924, though, Congress severely limited the number of immigrants allowed into the United States. Clear favoritism was shown to people from northern European countries. In 1965, Congress changed the law again. America's borders reopened to immigrants from all over the world, though quotas were set on the sending countries and priority went to people with family already in the United States.

The upshot of these legal changes has been that immigrants today are very different from their predecessors. In the 1970 census, 63 percent of immigrants (most of whom were admitted under the 1924 law) were born in Europe or Canada. In 2000, when most immigrants had been admitted under the 1965 law, only 14 percent of them were born in Europe, while 48 percent were born in Mexico, Central America, and the Caribbean, and 27 percent were born in Asia.

And today, 30 percent of immigrants are in America illegally, according to a study by the Pew Hispanic Forum.

(What you call immigrants without legal permission to be in the United States can be rhetorically loaded. Advocates of more open immigration have called them "undocumented workers." Jeffrey Passel's report for the Pew Hispanic Center referred to them as "unauthorized migrants." Critics have called them "illegal aliens" or worse. We will call them "illegal immigrants." All we intend from this label is that they are immigrants, and that they do not have legal permission to be in the United States. That label does not imply that there is anything "illegal" about them as human beings.)

Welfare Strain and Anchor Babies

The highest-profile immigration-related issue today centers around illegal immigrants. Unfortunately, the debate is littered with wrong perceptions. As *New York Times* reporter Daniel Altman put it, "Illegal immigrants do not just pick fruit, they do not just work off the books, they rarely earn less than the minimum wage and they may even be raising employment without harming incomes."

It's hard to know how many illegal immigrants are in the United States. They aren't usually interested in talking to government survey takers, after all. But a good recent estimate came from Jeffrey Passel in a research report for the Pew Hispanic Center. He concluded that there were 11.1 million illegal immigrants in 2005, split into 5.4 million adult males, 3.9 million adult females, and 1.8 million children. More than 75 percent of these illegal immigrants were from Mexico and other parts of Latin America. And 7.2 million illegal immigrants have jobs— about 5 percent of all U.S. workers.

Illegal immigrants get into the United States in one of two ways. Most "enter without inspection" by crossing a border (usually the Mexican border) without going through an official entry point. But between 25 and 40 percent enter lawfully on a tourist or other visa and then stay on past the visa's expiration date.

What jobs do illegal immigrants have? They are most common in jobs such as construction work, farm work, meat processing, grounds maintenance, housekeeping, and food service (mainly cooking and cleaning). According to Passel, 94 percent of illegal male immigrants work, compared to 86 percent of legal male immigrants and 83 percent of native-born men. (Female illegal immigrants are less likely to work than female legal immigrants and native-borns.)

Of course, this makes sense. People only move for a reason. Latin Americans come mainly for economic opportunity. So more men come to the United States illegally than women—and when they get here, they work.

Illegal immigrants are not usually forced to work at substandard wages. Economist Gordon Hanson of the University of California at San Diego reports that average wages for all Mexican immigrants were generally anywhere from $8–12 an hour, depending on age and education. Even though these numbers include earnings of legal immigrants, Hanson said there is not a large difference in pay between legal and illegal immigrants.

Critics of illegal immigration are everywhere. One example is Tom DeWeese, president of the American Policy Center. "Our nation is being flooded by people who don't care about our heritage or culture," he wrote on the APC's Web site.

> They have no allegiance to this country, and in fact, remain loyal to their home country. They choose not to learn our language and they ignore our laws. Our taxpayer-funded services are diminishing, as hospitals and schools are facing overcrowding and bankruptcy. This is no foundation on which to build our nation's future.

DeWeese thinks that the U.S. government should "stop providing U.S. taxpayer funded programs like hospital care, access to public schools, and welfare handouts. Plans to provide Social Security payments to illegals should never be considered. Stop granting automatic citizenship to babies born to illegal immigrants (known as 'anchor babies')."

Is DeWeese right about illegal immigrants? Let's start with the "anchor babies," a pejorative term used to describe children born in the United States to illegal aliens. DeWeese seems unhappy that the U.S. Constitution grants citizenship to these children. But his arguments against illegal immigrants don't hold up.

According to Passel's report, there are 1.8 million children who are illegal immigrants and another 3.1 million children born in the United States to illegal immigrant parents. Almost half of the adult illegal immigrants have no children at all in the United States. Among adult illegal immigrants, men outnumber women three-to-two. And the 9.3 million adult illegal immigrants are almost twice the number of their 4.9 million children. These facts don't support the idea that having a child with U.S.-born status is a main driver of illegal immigration.

In some parts of the country, hospitals and schools are certainly feeling financial strain from serving immigrants, legal and illegal. Admittedly, school costs are borne mainly by local governments. However, health care costs are offset by Medicaid and by Medicare's Disproportionate Share program. Illegal immigrants are not eligible for programs such as TANF, food stamps, WIC, and subsidized housing, though a household with at least one citizen can qualify. Even so, we saw in chapter 4 that these programs do not represent a large proportion of the federal budget.

Plus, since so many illegal immigrants work, many pay taxes that offset these costs—at least in part. Not just income taxes, either. They pay payroll taxes, sales taxes, property taxes on their homes (or via rent payments), gas taxes, and many more.

The Valenzuelas brought a baby with them to the United States and had another one while here. But they aren't looking for their U.S.-born child to serve as the family's anchor to America. Their anchor is that successful business they run, the one that allows them to pursue their own mobile version of the American Dream.

Lawbreakers

Most Americans learned the story in elementary school. The English government had imposed an import tax on tea in the American colonies. On November 28, 1773, a British cargo ship carrying tea had arrived in Boston Harbor. Colonists from Boston and surrounding towns told the ship owner that the tea was not to be unloaded and that they would pay no taxes.

On December 14, the ship owner asked the royal governor for permission to leave the harbor, since all cargo but the tea had been unloaded. The governor said no. Two evenings later, during another meeting of the colonists, the ship owner confirmed that the governor would not let the ship leave until the tea was unloaded. A voice in the gallery shouted, "Boston harbor a teapot tonight!" And a crowd headed out of Boston's Old South Meeting House toward the wharf. Sixty men boarded the British ship (plus two others that had arrived in the meantime) and tossed 342 kegs of tea into the harbor.

The Boston Tea Party drew strong reactions from the British crown and generated sympathy on both sides of the Atlantic for American self-rule. It stands as a watershed event in the founding of the United States.

Then there was the Woolworth lunch counter in Greensboro, North Carolina. During the Jim Crow era, African-Americans were not served there. So on February 1, 1960, four African-American freshmen from Greensboro's segregated North Carolina A&T College sat down at the lunch counter and placed an order. While Woolworth's employees did not make them leave the seats, they wouldn't serve the students either. The Greensboro Four stayed in those seats and returned the next day to "sit-in" again.

The Woolworth sit-in continued for several months, with hundreds of other students joining in and taking turns occupying seats at the lunch counter and standing in picket lines outside. It also inspired additional sit-ins in fifty-four cities across the South. And on July 25, 1960, Woolworth served African-Americans at that lunch counter for the first time ever. Civil rights activist James Farmer wrote, "With their very bodies they obstructed the wheels of injustice."

DeWeese says that illegal immigrants "ignore our laws" and don't care about "our heritage or culture." This attitude is central to the day-to-day rhetoric of opponents of illegal immigration, on talk radio, in TV commentaries, and in letters to the editor. But our heritage and culture are built on the likes of the Boston Tea Party and the Greensboro Four, where American heroes "ignored" laws that they thought were unjust.

The goals of illegal immigrants are a lot less lofty. The four Mexicans crossing the border with John Annerino weren't seeking to alter the course of national history. They only wanted what most Americans want—"a better life for themselves."

Saying that illegal immigrants are immoral because they are lawbreakers assumes that American immigration law is sensible and just. Yet, there are jobs for seven million illegal immigrants at the same time that the national unemployment rate is below 5 percent and the employment-to-adult-population ratio is near its all-time high. At a minimum, these facts suggest that the immigration quotas set by current law are too low and hardly sensible.

Have illegal immigrants broken American law? Yes. Then again, the Boston Tea Party and the Greensboro Four broke laws. The point is not that illegal immigrants are as heroic as these figures. Rather, it is that illegal immigrants are not immoral, just as the Boston Tea Party and the Greensboro Four were not.

Besides, contrary to urban myth, studies show that immigrants are no more likely to commit crimes than similar nativeborns. For example, in the journal *Social Forces*, criminologists John Hagan and Alberto Polloni recognized that Hispanic immigrants tend to be young, male, and single, all of which make them more likely to commit crimes. Once they controlled for these factors, Hagan and Polloni found that Hispanic immigrants were less likely to commit crimes than native-born Hispanics.

Fitting In

DeWeese is also wrong in saying that immigrants, legal or illegal, "have no allegiance" to the United States. Pradip Kothari certainly does. The Valenzuelas would like to be part of this country. And most immigrants manage to assimilate in much the same way as past immigrants have—a little bit at a time and over the course of a couple of generations.

Economic assimilation has been measured through both earnings and education. In general, says Cal-Berkeley economist David Card, first-generation immigrants never earn as much as native-born Americans with otherwise similar backgrounds. But the immigrants' American-born children do much better.

Writing in *Economic Journal*, Card showed how second-generation Americans generally get more education than otherwise similar third-or-higher-generation Americans. (Card defined a second-generation American as someone born in the United States to at least one foreign-born parent.) He also found that second-generation Americans earn more than those who have been in the United States for more generations.

This doesn't mean that a second-generation Mexican is more educated or better paid than a fifteenth-generation Anglo. It means that second-generation Mexicans are more educated and better paid than third-or-more-generation Mexicans just like them.

Even so, Card found that much of the educational gap across ethnic groups disappeared by the second generation. "Even sons of Mexican immigrants, whose fathers had 5.5 years of schooling less than native-born fathers in 1980 (7.3 years versus 12.8 years for native-born fathers) ended up with 12.2 years of schooling, closing 80% of the education gap faced by their fathers," he concluded.

And Mexicans who move to the United States are generally better educated than those who stay behind. As table 9.1 shows,

Mexican immigrants to the United States are more likely to have at least ten years of schooling than residents of Mexico.

TABLE 9.1	EDUCATIONAL ATTAINMENT OF WORKING-AGE MEXICANS IN 2000			
	Men		**Women**	
Highest Grade of Schooling	Residents of Mexico	Mexican Immigrants in U.S.	Residents of Mexico	Mexican Immigrants in U.S.
0–9	69.4%	60.1%	72.5%	62.0%
10–15	19.3%	35.0%	19.4%	33.2%
16+	11.3%	5.0%	8.0%	4.8%

Source: Gordon H. Hanson, "Illegal Migration from Mexico to the United States," *Journal of Economic Literature*, Dec. 2006, 897.

There is another way that immigrants are assimilating. And it will shock anyone who thinks nothing good can ever come of the search for corporate profits. It turns out that American companies' pursuit of profit has drawn many Hispanic illegal immigrants into mainstream economic life. Eleven million potential customers are just too hard to ignore, according to *Business Week*. So businesses have begun accepting a Mexican identification card called the *matrícula consular*. The *matrícula* is a photo ID issued by Mexican consulates in the United States. It serves as proof of Mexican citizenship. Other Latin American countries have begun to issue *matrículas* as well. (DeWeese is very unhappy with the growth of the *matrícula* as an acceptable form of identification in the United States.)

The *matrícula* is accepted to open bank accounts, obtain car financing, get cell-phone service, qualify for home mortgage loans, and more. By 2005, Wells Fargo had opened 525,000 *matrícula* accounts—6 percent of all of the bank's accounts. Blue Cross of California even sells health insurance to *matrícula* holders from desks located inside Mexican and Guatemalan consulates.

Kraft Foods—not wanting to miss a chance at a sale—donates workbooks to English-as-a-Second-Language (ESL) classes. The workbooks include instructions on how to redeem coupons in grocery stores for products such as Capri Sun drinks—made by Kraft.

"Corporations are helping, essentially, to bring a huge chunk of the underground economy into the mainstream," said *Business Week*. "By finding ways to treat illegals like any other consumers, companies are in effect legalizing—and legitimizing—millions of people who technically have no right to be in the U.S."

Taking Jobs Away from Americans?

The real question, though, is this: Do immigrants take jobs away from poor Americans and drive down wages for the rest? Basic supply-and-demand says that adding more workers to a market (an increase in supply) will lead to lower wages for all workers in that market. So if a large number of unskilled workers from Mexico seek construction jobs in the United States, then construction wages will fall, and some American construction workers may end up out of work. If many engineers from India or China come to the United States and seek jobs, then some engineers will be paid less and some American engineers may not find jobs. Of course, this assumes that all other things don't change—most notably, demand for workers.

It turns out that studies can't find any major effects of immigrants on either wages or native-born employment. At worst, the effects are negative but small. Immigrants may "take" a few American jobs and push wages down a little bit. But it's more likely that immigrants flow in because demand for workers is growing. Why? Because the American workforce is aging, and because American families are having fewer children. Fertility in the United States is barely at the replacement rate of just over two children per woman. Plus, about 75 percent of men aged twenty and up are already in the labor force; for women, the rate is about 60 percent. The unemployment rate in 2007 is well below 5 percent. When employers want to hire more workers, there aren't enough native-born Americans to choose from. Immigrants come to the United States because American employers need them.

American social-insurance programs need immigrant workers too. Social Security and Medicare mostly benefit the elderly, using taxes on workers. Americans are living longer today, which means that social-insurance costs are increasing. At the same time, post–Baby Boom generations have been smaller, so that there are fewer workers to support the growing elderly population. Immigrants are new workers who can help solve this imbalance across age groups.

And it's even possible that wages are growing as immigrants arrive. This is because human migration may naturally be accompanied by capital migration. According to Robert LaLonde of the University of Chicago, "Capital is a much more mobile factor than labor is, so if labor's moving in, you better believe that capital's not too far behind."

If he's right, then immigrants are taking jobs that wouldn't exist without them.

Skilled Immigrants Welcome

When Pradip Kothari opened his travel agency in the early 1980s, he was an innovator among Indian immigrants. At that time, most Indians in the United States preferred professional jobs, according to *Suburban Sahibs*. Kothari was in the vanguard of a new wave of Indian immigrants—the entrepreneurs.

A decade later, many immigrants were prospering as entrepreneurs. Immigrants helped found more than a quarter of all American engineering and technology start-ups between 1995 and 2005, according to a study by Vivek Wadhwa, an executive-in-residence at Duke University's Pratt School of Engineering.

The firms these immigrants helped to create have $52 billion in sales and employ 450,000 people. Almost all of these immigrant entrepreneurs held advanced university degrees, mostly in science, technology, engineering, and math.

According to Wadhwa, immigrants from India, the United Kingdom, China, Taiwan, Japan, and Germany are all better educated on average than native-born Americans. And Indian immigrants started more engineering and technology firms than the next four countries combined.

Bringing in and retaining highly skilled immigrants should be an important part of U.S.-immigration policy. Well-educated immigrants can contribute immediately to producing the high-end goods and services that the United States specializes in. They can help the United States to maintain its global advantage in technology. And they can provide the expanded tax base needed to keep our social-insurance programs afloat.

Strangers and Strange Lands

Attitudes such as Tom DeWeese's are not just troublesome from an economic standpoint. They also run afoul of biblical principles on the treatment of foreigners in our midst. How does denying citizenship to U.S.-born babies of illegal immigrants (as DeWeese and others would like to do) treat the foreigner properly? How does it keep them from feeling like strangers in a strange land?

When it comes to trade and immigration, a lot of people have good intentions to protect our own workers by prohibiting foreign goods from entering U.S.-consumer markets and keeping illegal immigrants out. They think these things will preserve jobs in fading industries and keep paychecks up.

They also think that refusing to buy the products of foreign sweatshops will help people overseas to attain a better life. But most of the evidence shows that trade is the path to a better life for people in poor countries and a source of increased prosperity for people in rich ones. It shows that immigrants contribute to the American economy in valuable ways.

Scripture calls Christians to welcome strangers and to reach out to strange lands. We can do this by helping immigrants among us: set up English classes, provide help in locating jobs and housing, welcome immigrant children into programs that develop their spiritual assets. Just welcoming immigrants into churches can help them assimilate into their new country.

Christian groups can also look out for both strangers and strange lands through public advocacy. They can push for freer trade while also keeping a close eye on the most egregious labor and environmental practices. They can preach the virtues of sensible immigration reform built around the need for good workers instead of reacting to fears of people who are different.

Like the Hebrews in Egypt, everyone living in the United States was once an alien here or has an ancestor who was. Even the Native Americans migrated here from Asia or Polynesia, according to the most recent anthropological research.

As the Bible teaches, do not oppress today's aliens, for we were once aliens ourselves.

10. IS CAPITALISM RUINING THE ENVIRONMENT?

Matthew Sleeth is haunted by the memory of a little girl named Etta.

Eight years old and wearing a green bathing suit with a smiling whale on it, Etta had been running through a sprinkler with her brother on a hot, hazy, and humid day when she suffered a severe asthma attack. An ambulance took her to the emergency room, where Sleeth was working as a young doctor in the 1990s.

When Etta arrived, her airway was almost completely closed. Sleeth and his colleagues sprang into action. Sleeth put a mask over her face and tried to push air into her lungs by compressing an air bag. No luck. So he began threading a tube down her throat in hopes of getting air into Etta's lungs.

As he started, Sleeth looked down at the frightened girl and held her hand. As he recounted in a recent issue of *Guideposts* magazine, he told her, "I won't let anything bad happen to you, sweetheart."

But Sleeth says that he broke that promise. He and the other doctors could not save Etta. They could not get her to breathe.

Despite their best efforts, she died right there in the ER.

Sleeth eventually became chief of an ER at a small hospital in Maine. As the years went by, he noticed a disturbing trend. More and more patients were suffering from asthma and other chronic illnesses. He began to suspect that it wasn't just his patients that were sick. Something seemed wrong with the very air they breathed. That suspicion was confirmed by a report from the Harvard University School of Public Health.

Scientists at Harvard had been studying the effects of air pollution from older, coal-fired power plants on residents of New England, eastern New York, and New Jersey. They concluded that emissions from two Massachusetts power plants—the Salem Harbor plant and the Brayton Point plant—could be linked "to more than 43,000 asthma attacks and nearly 300,000 incidents of upper respiratory symptoms per year in the region," according to Harvard's announcement about the study. The study also estimated that "159 premature deaths per year could be attributed to this pollution."

Thinking of patients such as Etta, Sleeth decided he wanted to do more to help them. Instead of only treating their symptoms, Sleeth wanted to treat the cause of their diseases. That meant doing something about air pollution.

He turned to his faith to do that. That led to a conversion, one that Sleeth detailed in both *Guideposts* and a book called *Serve God, Save the Planet.*

He started with prayer and Bible study. "I needed guidance," Sleeth recalled in *Guideposts*. "I found myself praying more intensely than ever. I thought about the Psalms, where I'd read, as a child, that God makes the rain fall, that he hears the cry of a hungry blackbird. That he sends the snow and wind, and knows each star by name."

While praying, Sleeth began to ask God what he should do. He felt God telling him to treat the planet in the same way that he would treat a patient. The first step was changing his own life—and the way his family of four lived. The Sleeths owned a four-bedroom, 3,500-square-foot house and a pair of cars, and more stuff than they knew what to do with. The more time Sleeth spent in the Bible, the more he came to believe that his lifestyle didn't fit Jesus's teaching.

In an interview with *Grist* magazine, Sleeth described his conversion from an affluent lifestyle to one in which Jesus's teaching came first. "Christ says, give half of everything you have to the Lord and follow me," Sleeth said.

> If you have two coats, give one away, and first seek the Kingdom of Heaven; don't store up treasures on earth. And between that and where I was in life as a doctor was a huge gap. It also says to change yourself first, and then change somebody else. Don't see the speck in the other person's eye, but get the two-by-four out of your own.

The Sleeths sold their McMansion and moved into a house that was half as big as their old place. Though the new house was about the same size as their old garage, they felt happier in it. When the Sleeths realized that they consumed the equivalent of 4,800 gallons of gasoline a year to power their lifestyle—the average Italian family consumes about 1,300 gallons a year—they sold off their cars and bought a hybrid. They installed energy-saving lightbulbs, turned off lights wherever they could, and cut their trash output down from two barrels a week to one trash bag every two weeks. They gave up their dishwasher and clothes dryer. They bought and consumed less and were happier for it. Convinced that more Christians could do the same—and in doing so make the world a healthier place to live—Sleeth quit his job and began traveling the country, urging Christians to help save the planet.

The Earth Might Warm Up a Little Bit

On the other side of the Atlantic, Sir John Houghton was doing much the same thing. A lifelong evangelical Christian, Houghton is one of the most prestigious meteorologists in the world. In 1967, he gave a talk to the British Association for the Advancement of Science about a little-known phenomenon called "global warming." Houghton told *Creation Care* magazine that, at the time, he didn't think global warming was much to worry about. "We realized the earth might warm up a little bit, by one degree 'C' [Celsius] or something of that order, but we had no idea how dangerous that might be. That didn't come until later."

As time went by, Houghton and other scientists became more and more concerned about global warming, especially the effects it might have on poor countries. In 1983, he was named general director of the Meteorological Office—the national weather service for the United Kingdom. Using computer models and data about the skyrocketing use of fossil fuels, Houghton realized that global warming, also known as "climate change," was happening faster than anyone had predicted.

When the Intergovernmental Panel on Climate Change (IPCC) was formed in 1987, Houghton was put in charge of scientific assessment for the group. By the early 1990s, they had reached enough consensus to understand that global warming was happening fast and that one of the major causes was human activity—the carbon dioxide being spewed into the atmosphere when fossil fuels are burned. In 1992, world leaders, including President George H. W. Bush, gathered in Rio de Janeiro for a climate-change convention—known as the Earth Summit—and signed a framework document on the need to address global warming.

"What does that convention say?" Houghton asked *Creation Care*. "It says that although we haven't got absolute certainty, we have enough information, enough knowledge with which to act and we should be acting now. And that was in 1992."

Convinced that American Christians, if properly motivated to care for God's creation, could be a powerful force for tackling global warming and other environmental issues, Houghton began to build relationships with evangelical leaders. He befriended Rick Cizik of the National Association of Evangelicals (NAE), which led to an invitation to speak to evangelical leaders. Houghton presented most of the findings of the IPCC. The main points were this: Climate change caused by human beings is real, and it will hurt millions of poor people.

Those meetings led to the Evangelical Climate Initiative, which issued a statement in 2006 known as "Climate Change: An Evangelical Call to Action." Among the signers were Leith Anderson, president of the NAE; Clive Calver, former president of World Relief; Luis Cortes, president of Esperanza USA and organizer of the National Hispanic Prayer Breakfast; *Christianity Today* editor David Neff; Jim Wallis of *Sojourners* magazine; and Rick Warren, pastor of Saddleback Church and author of *The Purpose Driven Life*.

The statement reads:

> Over the last several years many of us have engaged in study, reflection, and prayer related to the issue of climate change (often called "global warming"). For most of us, until recently this has not been treated as a pressing issue or major priority. Indeed, many of us have required considerable convincing before becoming persuaded that climate change is a real problem and that it ought to matter to us as Christians.

To support their claims, the signers drew on three biblical principles:

- Christians must care about climate change because we love God the Creator and Jesus our Lord, through whom and for

whom the creation was made. This is God's world, and any
damage that we do to God's world is an offense against God
Himself (Genesis 1; Psalm 24; Colossians 1:16).

■ Christians must care about climate change because we are
called to love our neighbors, to do unto others as we would
have them do unto us, and to protect and care for the least of
these as though each was Jesus Christ Himself (Matthew
22:34–40; Matthew 7:12; Matthew 25:31–46).

■ Christians, noting the fact that most of the climate change
problem is human induced, are reminded that when God
made humanity He commissioned us to exercise stewardship
over the earth and its creatures. Climate change is the latest
evidence of our failure to exercise proper stewardship, and
constitutes a critical opportunity for us to do better (Genesis
1:26–28).

Can Christians Make a Difference?

Like Houghton and Sleeth, millions of Christians are concerned about pollution and global warming. But it's hard to
know how to respond. These issues seem beyond the ability of
any individual to make a difference. Some Christians have taken
steps that they hope will help.

Sleeth's family chose to embrace a simpler life. An evangelical Christian, Sleeth calls this "putting the *conserve* back into
conservatism." But it's not just evangelicals who can "go green."
American Christians disagree on many things, but almost all
agree that God created the Earth and put human beings in
charge of taking care of it. The Earth is on loan—it belongs to
God, not to us. One of our jobs is to pass the Earth on in usable
condition to future generations until the Lord returns.

While one family probably can't make a big impact, tens of
millions of Christians can. If all kinds of Christians—evangelicals

and Pentecostals, mainliners and Catholics—drove less, bought fuel-efficient cars, installed energy-saving lightbulbs, recycled their trash at home and at church (or made less of it), gave up their dishwashers and clothes dryers, it would have a profound effect.

To try to convince more people to embrace this conservation lifestyle, some Christians—and non-Christians as well—have decided to treat pollution like a sin and polluters like sinners. That's in part what the Evangelical Climate Initiative does. So does another statement: "An Evangelical Declaration on the Care of Creation."

> As followers of Jesus Christ, committed to the full authority of the Scriptures, and aware of the ways we have degraded creation, we believe that biblical faith is essential to the solution of our ecological problems . . . Because we worship and honor the Creator, we seek to cherish and care for the creation. Because we have sinned, we have failed in our stewardship of creation. Therefore we repent of the way we have polluted, distorted, or destroyed so much of the Creator's work.

If we view polluters as sinners, the obvious conclusion is to punish them and to make them atone for their sins. This can be done through regulations that restrict how much companies (or individuals) can pollute, and by making polluters clean up their messes.

Guilt-Free Pollution

Viewing pollution as a sin—at least when it comes to global warming—has led many Americans and Europeans to look for ways to atone for their transgressions. One popular solution has been to buy "carbon offsets."

Global warming is caused by greenhouse gases, primarily

carbon dioxide. So people have started buying carbon offsets to pay for their sin of polluting.

These function a bit like medieval indulgences. Consumers and companies estimate their "carbon footprint"—equivalent to the amount of pollution they create by driving, flying, using electricity at home, and so on. Then they buy offsets to cancel out that footprint. This might involve planting trees to absorb carbon dioxide or investing in alternative energy, such as wind or solar power. Kimberly Lisagor of *Mother Jones* magazine calls it "Paying for my hot air."

Lisagor, a journalist who rides her bike as much as possible and tries to live a green lifestyle, also travels a lot for her work. Airplane travel, it turns out, is like sinning twice—modern jets spew large amounts of greenhouse gases into the air and deposit those gases high in the atmosphere, where they stay for a long time. (Greenhouse gases generated closer to the ground can be more easily absorbed by trees or by the oceans.)

When Lisagor calculated her carbon footprint, she was appalled. According to the Earth Day Network's online lifestyle quiz, she was a mega-polluter. Her quiz results said, "If everyone lived like you, we would need 6.2 planets."

"Humbled and mildly indignant," Lisagor wrote in *Mother Jones*, "I did what any American consumer would do: looked to buy my way out of the problem." She shopped around for carbon offsets and found the best price online (estimates ranged from $180 to $408 a year). Then, faced with either giving up air travel or buying offsets—and convinced that the latter actually did some good—she settled for offsets.

Still, she felt that buying carbon offsets was somehow wrong. "The whole idea of atonement by credit card seems counterintuitive," she wrote. "It's as if we're saying polluting is okay, as long as you can afford to pay."

Lisagor put her finger on one of the downsides of carbon offsets. They can actually encourage more pollution. That appears to be the case for former vice president Al Gore. The day after *An Inconvenient Truth*, the global-warming film starring Gore, won several Oscars, news leaked out about his enormous electrical bills. In 2006, Gore's estate (which includes a pool house) used up more than 221,000 kilowatt hours—more than twenty times the national average.

Gore paid close to $30,000 for gas and electricity in 2006, according to public records collected by the Tennessee Center for Policy Research. Gore's spokesperson admitted that the figures were accurate. In defense, the spokesperson argued that Gore and his family purchased offsets to zero out their carbon footprint.

Sergey Brin, one of the founders of Google, has also used carbon offsets with embarrassing results. *The New York Times* reported that Brin used offsets to alleviate guilt over using the company's private Boeing 767 jet.

The reason that offsets may actually encourage pollution is that they mix up the decision to pollute with the decision to cut pollution. The rationale behind offsets is basically morality-based. Do something bad (pollute), and redeem yourself by doing something good (the offset). And clever sellers of offsets can profit from the guilt.

But polluting is a problem whether you offset it or not. And planting trees is a good thing even if you don't pollute. The two acts—polluting and offsetting—are separate. Offsets don't buy redemption. And viewing pollution as a sin ignores some basic truths about the nature of pollution and where it comes from— truths that an economic perspective can help us to understand.

An Optimal Level of Pollution?

Economists don't think much about sin. Instead, they think about "externalities." Before we talk about externalities, however, it might help to think a little bit about the nature of pollution.

No one likes to pollute. We don't do it on purpose—for the

mere sake of polluting. Instead, it is a by-product of good things we do. Families, for example, need to eat. So the United States and other developed nations buy food from the grocery store and bring it home. But that act of buying groceries produces pollution: the packaging needed to get the food safely home, the gas burned on the drive to the store and back, the leftover trash at the grocery store when all the food is unloaded from delivery trucks.

Even if we raised everything at home, there would still be leftover trash. There would still be wheat stalks we don't want to eat, or animal carcasses left over once the meat has been butchered, or the exhaust from our tractors. Not to mention the manure from the animals we raised.

We don't make trash for its own sake—we make trash while making something else. In the same way, power plants don't make pollution. They make the electricity that has improved our standard of living, and pollution is a by-product of the electricity. The same is true for any other producer. Paper mills, oil refineries, food processors—these all make things that are good and useful, but they also make pollution.

Recognizing that pollution is an unavoidable part of producing things that are good has some profound implications. First, it means determining the *optimal level of pollution*. Conceptually, society should want to produce good things—such as electricity—up to the point where the last bit of electricity generated creates benefits equal to the social cost of the last bit of pollution simultaneously produced. To generate any more electricity would mean that society loses more due to pollution than it gains from the extra electricity. In other words, there's a constant balancing act between creating things we need—such as food or electricity—and limiting the things we don't need, such as pollution.

The second implication follows from the first. Because some amount of pollution is unavoidable in making things that are good, *the optimal level of pollution is not zero*. To get zero pollution, we would either have to produce nothing or spend more on cleanup than the product is worth. The trick is determining the optimal level of pollution.

Externalities

Instead of treating pollution as a sin, economists treat it as an externality, or an unwanted by-product. Pollution is a problem because no one wants it. That's not always the case with by-products, as some are useful. Consider the husks on the pineapples sold by the Dole Company. When we buy Dole's canned pineapples, we don't want the tough husk in our can. From a pineapple-eater's perspective, the husk is an undesirable by-product. But the husks can be used for cattle feed. Unlike pollution, the husks are not a problem because cattle ranchers want them.

But nobody wants pollution. Just as important, pollution is a problem because it gets dumped onto people who have no say in whether it gets produced. It's what economists call an externality—a cost (or benefit) from a market transaction felt by people outside the transaction.

For example, when a paper mill sells paper to customers, the price and quantity are set by the paper mill and its customers. The people who live downstream from the mill have no say, even though they have to deal with pollution and the cleanup costs. Absent government regulations, neither the mill nor the paper buyers have to pay for cleanup of downstream pollution. To the mill owners and its customers, pollution is free.

The same kind of externality exists whenever we drive our cars down the highway. We pay for gas, tolls, tires, maintenance, and even car insurance. But the air pollution we create is free. It doesn't cost us anything, and so why not continue to pollute? Certainly, we can decide to pollute less because it's the right thing to do. But we have no incentive—outside of our own conscience—to stop polluting.

To limit the effects of a negative externality such as pollution, economists look for ways to make the paper mill or the customer take the externality's cost into account. This is called "internalizing the externality." One of the best ways this has been done is with tradable pollution permits.

A Right to Pollute?

In the late 1980s, acid rain was constantly in the news. And the news was almost all bad.

Maple, red spruce, and Fraser fir trees in Vermont were dying. Wild trout in Virginia were disappearing because the rivers they swam in were becoming "acidified," as the *Washington Post* put it. Rivers and streams up and down the Atlantic seaboard were facing the same fate. Rockfish, shad, and herring populations were shrinking in Chesapeake Bay. A professor from Colorado had even discovered a "toxic form of moss," which thrived on the chemicals from acid rain and killed off trees and other plant life.

The main culprit in acid rain was sulfur dioxide (or SO_2), which—along with nitrous oxide—is one of the main gases released by coal-burning power plants. (You may recall from high school chemistry class that water in the clouds mixes with these gases and turns into sulfuric or nitric acid.) But eliminating those SO_2 emissions was expected to cost billions. Estimates were as high as $1,000 per ton of pollution. So power-plant owners balked at air-pollution regulation for years.

Then, in the late 1980s, President George H. W. Bush's administration proposed a novel idea, known as a cap-and-trade system. The federal government would set a cap on the total SO_2 pollution it would allow, then issue permits to companies. The permits gave them permission to emit a certain quantity of SO_2. In addition, if a company found ways to cut SO_2 emissions, it could sell off its unused permits to the highest bidder.

This used a market to sort out the firms that could reduce

SO_2 cheaply from those who couldn't. Different polluters faced different costs of lowering SO_2 emissions. Some could lower SO_2 cheaply. These low-cost emissions reducers could pay to reduce SO_2 and sell off their permits for more than they had paid to eliminate the pollution. While low-cost emissions reducers made a profit by selling their permits, the high-cost polluters also saved money because permits cost them less than reducing emissions. Meanwhile, the government's overall SO_2 emissions target was met.

In effect, greed became green. Cutting pollution was profitable. Since polluting less made money, firms got creative and found their own ways to cut SO_2 emissions. This was possible because polluters got a limited right to pollute. Instead of being a social evil, pollution became a commodity to be bought and sold, which internalized the externality.

The cap-and-trade system became legal in 1990, when Congress passed the Clean Air Act. It took awhile to get the details straight, but in 1992, the Wisconsin Power and Light company sold the first pollution permits under the system, trading ten thousand SO_2 credits for somewhere between $2.5 and $4 million dollars.

The idea of selling pollution rights, as you might guess, was not popular. *The Nation* labeled the cap-and-trade system "The Stink Market," and wondered why the government hadn't set up similar markets for murders. The magazine's editors were repulsed by the idea of turning "toxic fumes into gold by selling pollution rights."

Chris Blythe, a spokesperson for the Citizen's Utility Board, a Wisconsin consumer-protection group, was equally blunt. "Clean air should be protected, not traded and sold like a used car," Blythe told the *Milwaukee Journal Sentinel*. "What's next? The L.A. police department trying to buy civil rights credits from Wisconsin?" (Such objections ignore the reality that the optimal level of pollution is not zero. Presumably, the optimal level of murders and civil-rights violations *is* zero.)

Despite its unseemly nature, selling pollution rights worked, at least for SO_2. The Environmental Protection Agency had set a goal of reducing sulfur-dioxide emissions by 40 percent in ten years—a goal it exceeded with ease. In 1998, for example, a reporter from *The Boston Globe* followed Donald Buso, a New Hampshire scientist, as he snowmobiled up to Watershed No. 6, a remote stream in the White Mountains. For two decades, Buso had been testing water from the stream as it became more and more contaminated by acid rain.

On a winter morning in 1998, he found something remarkable. As Michael Kranish of *The Globe* reported, "Buso found that the level of acidity in the precipitation was one of the lowest recorded during his 23 years of work here—an astounding 200 times lower than the worst measurement during the same period. 'This is just pure water,' Buso marvels again and again, as if such purity is an impossibility."

What's almost as remarkable as the success of the Clean Air Act in controlling SO_2 was its cost. Initial cost estimates for reducing sulfur dioxide were around $1,000 per ton. In actuality, the costs were only about one-tenth of that.

Kranish also reported how the cap-and-trade system helped clean up the General John M. Gavin power plant in Cheshire, Ohio, one of the dirtiest coal plants in the United States. With a smokestack more than 1,100 feet high, the Gavin plant spewed pollution that reached all the way to New England. In 1990, the Gavin plant emitted 384,000 tons of SO_2 each year. And its owners fiercely opposed the Clean Air Act, claiming it would ruin them and devastate Cheshire's economy.

But after the act passed, Gavin's owners found a solution. Knowing that they could profit by reducing pollution, they installed $650 million worth of scrubbers in the smokestack, which reduced the plant's emissions to 68,000 tons a year. That's an annual reduction of 300,000 tons in annual pollution.

Gavin's owners then sold off their excess permits to pay for the improvements.

In short, the Clean Air Act worked. Its biggest shortcoming was not including nitrous oxide or carbon dioxide—two other power-plant emissions—in cap-and-trade systems. Those two gases continue to be a problem.

Greg Easterbrook, in an online interview with *The Atlantic Monthly*, described why the Clean Air Act worked, and why a similar approach might work for global warming.

"Once people have a profit incentive you're going to find a huge outpouring of creativity on the part of engineers coming up with technical ideas and business people coming up with entrepreneurial ideas. But the last thing you want is for government to try to pick winners and losers in an industry," he said.

> The government's track record in energy research is pitiful. If you look at the billions of dollars that have been spent since the first Arab oil crunch of 1974, in the '70s and '80s we were spending eight or nine billion dollars a year (stated in today's dollars) on federal subsidized energy research, and if anything useful came out of that research I'm sure not aware of it. All the breakthroughs in pollution reduction and energy efficiency—the things that actually work in the marketplace—have come at the behest of private entrepreneurs and engineers who are seeking profit. And so what we need to do now is create a profit motive for greenhouse gas reduction and apart from that, government should stay out of it.

What about China?

Many critics point to environmental damage as a reason to oppose globalization. Does economic growth in developing countries such as China threaten the environment? The answer is yes and no.

As China has gotten richer, it has also gotten dirtier. China is now second only to the United States in total carbon-dioxide emissions. (China also has about five times as many people as the United States.) And China may well pass the United States in total carbon-dioxide emissions in 2009, reported *The Guardian* of London in April 2007.

China has grown rapidly, and hundreds of millions of people are shaking off poverty because of it. But the growth is being built with coal-powered electricity, which has made China a much more polluted place. Similar trends are occurring in India and many other developing countries.

How serious is pollution in China? According to Robert Lee Hotz of *The Wall Street Journal*, Chinese pollution has effects around the globe. Chinese factories and power plants emit carbon and sulfate particles. These get caught up in dust clouds that sweep in from China's western deserts, and the mixture blows out to the Pacific Ocean. These plumes of dust and pollutants "can be wider than the Amazon and deeper than the Grand Canyon," wrote Hotz. And atmospheric physicist V. Ramanathan of the Scripps Institution of Oceanography told the *Journal* that "there are times when [the pollution] covers the entire Pacific Ocean basin like a ribbon bent back and forth."

"On some days, almost a third of the air over Los Angeles and San Francisco can be traced directly to Asia. With it comes up to three-quarters of the black carbon particulate pollution that reaches the West Coast," Hotz said.

Pollution of this magnitude needs to be dealt with. But how? Keeping poor countries poor is neither a feasible nor a desirable way to reduce the environmental impact of their growth. What else can be done? Matthew Clarke, an economist at Australia's Deakin University, says that rich countries should help poorer countries adopt cleaner and more efficient electricity-generation technology. As he wrote in the *Canberra Times*, that will require selling them better technology, probably at a reduced (and possibly subsidized) price.

China, for example, has relatively inefficient coal-fired power plants. As Greg Easterbrook pointed out in his interview with *The Atlantic Monthly*, a Chinese power plant burns twice as much coal and releases twice as much greenhouse gas to produce the same electricity as a plant in the United States.

"If American capital and expertise did nothing in the next 20 years except raise the efficiency of Chinese coal-fired power plants—if that's the only thing we did," he said, "it would be probably the single greatest contribution to slowing the rate of greenhouse gas accumulation that anybody could make in the world. It would certainly exceed any possible reform here in the United States."

In the meantime, though, nobody likes to breathe dirty air. When the United States got rich enough, we bought back a cleaner environment with costly but effective government regulations. The same should happen in the rest of the world at some point. But at best, that is probably decades away.

Until then, harm to the environment may be one of the costs of getting people out of poverty around the world. The best hope is to help poor countries burn their coal more cleanly as they escape poverty.

Etta

Power plants operating in a market spewed out pollutants, killing a little girl named Etta. Markets also helped the government reduce emissions of sulfur dioxide far more than was thought possible. Today, markets are helping people around the world improve their lives. These markets are being accompanied by more pollution, creating new health hazards.

So is capitalism ruining the environment? Perhaps. But it also may help save it.

In the spring of 2006, with gas prices approaching $3 a gallon, ExxonMobil had a public-relations crisis. With public outrage going off the charts over the cost of filling up, the oil giant reported a first-quarter profit of $8.4 billion. (Retail giant Wal-Mart, for comparison, reported just over $11 billion in profit for the *entire year* in 2006.) While profit reports usually get positive press, this one provoked outrage.

Members of Congress interrupted their discussion of funding for the war in Iraq to berate oil companies. The Senate Finance Committee went even further, according to *The Washington Post*, and planned to audit the tax records of fifteen oil companies. "We're seeing record profits and significant executive compensation in the oil and gas industry," committee chairman Charles E. Grassley (R-Iowa) told the *Post*. "I want to make sure the oil companies aren't taking a speed pass by the tax man."

The Senate Judiciary Committee approved a proposed new law treating the oil production quotas set by the Organization of Petroleum Exporting Countries (OPEC) as antitrust violations. The law would have also made mergers of oil companies more difficult to pass antitrust muster. "What you have today is an oligopoly, effectively, and I think it's a disaster for the American people," Senator Dianne Feinstein said.

"People are hopping mad," Tim Russert, host of *Meet the Press*, said in an online interview before hosting a show on oil prices. "NBC News and *The Wall Street Journal* did a poll that shows more people are concerned about gas prices than Iran having a nuclear weapon. It's just spiked in terms of the national consciousness."

Since 2001, Americans have been outraged, angry, or at least very annoyed by the price of gas. In the summer of 2007, the national average price for a gallon of regular unleaded gasoline crossed the $3 mark for the first time. Gas prices seem higher than ever before. It doesn't help that we see these seemingly outrageous prices plastered on signs at every street corner.

Gas prices have been high before, especially once we adjust for inflation. Figure 11.1 shows the inflation-adjusted price of a gallon of regular unleaded going back to 1973, around the time of the first OPEC price shock. The real price of gas was a little bit higher back in 1979–1981, following the second big OPEC price shock. After that, the United States enjoyed a period of lower prices, dropping as low as $1.21 (in 2007 dollars) in February 1999. Even over the last three years, the real price of gas has varied over a range of 80 cents, from $2.30 to $3.10.

Why are gas prices this high, and why do they fluctuate so much? The most popular answer is company greed. And this answer comes with a simple solution: the oil companies can either cut their prices or be punished. But things, as you might expect, are never that simple.

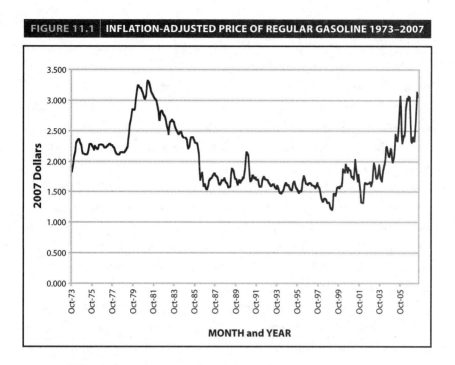

FIGURE 11.1 | INFLATION-ADJUSTED PRICE OF REGULAR GASOLINE 1973–2007

Supply and Demand

Gas prices are driven mostly by supply and demand. This is true for the market for crude oil—which is the main input used in refining gasoline—and in the market for gasoline. Lately, supply and demand have favored oil companies.

Let's start with the global market for crude oil. According to the federal Energy Information Agency (the EIA), almost 70 percent of the world's proven crude-oil reserves are in countries that belong to OPEC. As a result, the OPEC countries have a lot of power over how much crude oil is produced, and historically, OPEC has kept the supply of oil from growing too fast. These days, however, OPEC's production is about 92 percent of its total sustainable capacity, according to EIA data. Even if OPEC wanted to open the spigots, it's not clear that it could. Overall, the supply of crude oil is only growing slowly.

The demand for crude oil has been growing much faster than the supply. Economic growth—especially in China and India—has led to more demand for crude oil, as well as for all other forms of energy. When demand grows faster than supply, prices go up. Mix in concerns over political instability in the Middle East—complicated by the U.S. presence in Iraq—and you get the high crude-oil prices that global markets have been experiencing in recent years.

Of course, we put gasoline in our cars, not crude oil. Refineries convert crude oil into a variety of products, including gasoline. The higher price of crude oil drives up the cost of making gasoline. In the economist's basic supply-and-demand model, a higher-priced input means a decrease in supply—which drives up the price of gas.

In addition, there has been damage to refining capacity in the United States—Hurricanes Katrina and Rita in 2005 damaged refineries along the Gulf Coast, and a fire damaged the BP refinery in Whiting, Indiana. These were additional decreases in supply, and gasoline production could barely keep up with demand. As the demand went up and the supply didn't, the price followed the basic laws of economics—it went up.

Many Blends, Many Prices

One Saturday in August 2007, a gallon of regular unleaded in Waco, Texas, sold for around $2.60. A hundred miles north, in the Dallas–Fort Worth metro area, gas was fifteen to twenty cents higher per gallon. This variation in prices happens in big cities and nearby smaller cities all over America. But why?

Some variation is natural, even within the same town. Traffic patterns, the number of nearby stations, whether a station has a convenience store or not—these things and more affect how much a station charges for a gallon of gas.

But there is one factor that unexpectedly makes gas more expensive in Dallas than in Waco, or more in Chicago than in Peoria. Clean air.

In an effort to reduce pollution from cars, federal and state governments have imposed an array of regulations on the gas cars use. As a result, there are seventeen different blends of gasoline used across the country, according to the American Petroleum Institute.

If all gas were the same, and if gas prices were higher in Dallas than in Waco, gas station owners would send their gas to Dallas and sell it there for more money. The shift of supply from Waco to Dallas would lower prices in Dallas and increase them in Waco. This is how prices tend to even out across different cities.

But because of stricter air-pollution rules in Dallas, the gas sold in Waco can't be sold in Dallas. Gas prices are higher in Dallas than in Waco, and they stay that way because air-pollution rules make it illegal to substitute one for the other.

Where Has All the Money Gone?

With gas prices going up since 2001, who has pocketed the proceeds? The EIA says that in 2005, when the national average price of a gallon of regular unleaded was $2.27, about $1.20 went to the crude-oil producer. The rest was split among refining costs and profit (about forty-three cents per gallon), state and federal taxes (also about forty-three cents), and distribution and marketing (about twenty-one cents). Since oil companies earn most of the profit on crude-oil production and refining, they have made a lot of money. ExxonMobil, for example, had profits of nearly $40 billion in 2006—more than an 11 percent profit margin.

Ironically, the people who sell the gas don't profit much when prices go up. Gas stations earn about two to three cents per gallon in profit, according to the National Association of Convenience Stores. David Malik, who owns seven gas stations in and around

Seattle, told *The Seattle Times* that he "earns about as much on a can of Coke as he does on a typical 10-gallon purchase of gas."

In fact, most gas stations make their money on their convenience stores. Store owners keep their profit margins on gas low so that people will come into the store to buy the Coke, the cigarettes, and all of the other more profitable items offered inside.

Rising prices and shrinking profits—at least at the bottom of the food chain—convinced at least one gas station owner to throw in the towel. Angry at losing money running a Shell station while the corporate office was awash in profits, Bob Oyster gave up. He paid too much for gas from his supplier, and—to add insult to injury—got a notice that the rent had gone up on his station near the Golden Gate Bridge. Because Oyster didn't have room to expand, he couldn't add a convenience store to generate higher profit. "All I've got is gas and cigarettes," he told the *San Francisco Chronicle*. "And you can't sell that many cigarettes."

Are Gas Prices Too Low?

Despite the public outcry against soaring gas prices, a surprising number of respected economists think that prices need to be higher—mainly because of the carbon-dioxide-emissions externality created by car exhaust. Since the 1920s, economists have recognized that imposing a tax is one way to internalize an externality. A tax on gasoline can have this effect for carbon-dioxide emissions from cars, argues Steve Levitt, the University of Chicago economics professor and coauthor of *Freakonomics*.

Gas is much more expensive in other countries than in the United States, mostly because of taxes. As recently as 2004, gas was under $2 a gallon. For most of the rest of the world, even $3 a gallon is a bargain-basement price. In the summer of 2007, gas in London was $6.65 per gallon and $6.52 in Paris. It was $6.06 in Seoul, $4.17 in Mumbai, and $5.62 in Rome.

Levitt believes that Americans drive too much because gas prices are relatively low compared to the rest of the world. On his *Freakonomics* blog, he points to three major externalities from driving: "a) My driving increases congestion for other drivers; b) I might crash into other cars or pedestrians; c) My driving contributes to global warming." A higher gas tax would address all three.

Another economist who agrees with Levitt is Greg Mankiw, the Harvard professor who served as chairman of President George W. Bush's Council of Economic Advisors from 2003–2005. Mankiw thinks that the gas tax should be raised by a dollar per gallon over a ten-year period—ten cents a year.

Many economists and business leaders believe that gas prices need to be higher to get Americans to drive smaller cars. As Mike Kelly wrote in *Business Week*, "Most consumers won't trade in their Ford Expeditions, Toyota Sequoias, and Chevy Tahoes until gasoline moves permanently north of $4 per gallon."

The quickest way to increase gas prices is to raise gas taxes—something even the heads of U.S. automakers have pushed for. "Every place else we operate," William Clay Ford Jr., then head of Ford Motor Company, told *The New York Times* in 2004, "fuel prices are very high relative to here and customers get used to it, but they get used to it by having a smaller vehicle, a more efficient vehicle."

G. Richard Wagoner Jr., the chairman and chief executive of GM, told the *Times* the same thing. "If you want people to consume something less, the simplest thing to do is price it more dearly," he said. "And there is just no track record of sustainable success in the United States of doing that, versus Germany, for example, which just regularly says, 'Oh, we have a budget deficit; we're going to raise the fuel taxes by 10 pfennigs, or euros, or whatever,' and do that. And I think that's the rub."

Then again, higher gas prices are felt throughout the economy. The price of gas affects the cost of every good that is carried by a truck, which is most everything. Higher gas prices can fuel higher inflation and reductions in the GDP, as the United States saw in the late 1970s and (to a lesser degree) in the last few years. So raising the gas tax should not be done cavalierly—or too quickly.

A higher gas tax would also be regressive, meaning that it would be a larger portion of a poor person's income than a wealthy person's. Mankiw admits that this is true, and suggests that the revenue from a higher gas tax should be used to reduce other regressive taxes, such as payroll taxes.

But some economists are skeptical that a higher gas tax would be accompanied by lower taxes elsewhere. "My own guess is that the increased revenue from a higher gasoline tax would be more likely to finance additional government spending, just as it does in Europe," wrote Martin Feldstein—another Harvard economist and chairman of President Reagan's Council of Economic Advisors—in a *Wall Street Journal* editorial.

Higher gas taxes would have an uneven impact across regions of the country. As business columnist Daniel Gross wrote in the online magazine *Slate*, higher gas taxes would have less impact in places where people already heavily use mass transit—places such as New York, New Jersey, Maryland, and Connecticut. The larger impact would be felt in wide-open places with lower population densities. America's smaller cities can't create cost-effective substitutes for driving—for example, mass transit networks and carpool lanes are not sensible in less-congested metropolitan areas with under five hundred thousand people.

In the end, voters are not likely to agree that gas prices should be higher. But if Americans think that imports of crude oil should be cut, cars should be smaller, and auto emissions should be reduced, then higher gas taxes can accomplish all three.

Bottled Water, Pumping Gas

Every so often, a local TV news crew will do a story on rising gas prices. "Why are they going up?" they always ask. Some economist *du jour's* answer is basically the same—it's supply and demand. From story to story, the particular things affecting supply or demand will change. A refinery fire here, a pipeline problem there, a holiday weekend coming up—these things and more might help explain why gas is twenty-two cents more today than it was four weeks ago.

But the news reports like to go one step further—to the man (or woman) at the pumps. Mixed in with all the other camera shots—the reporter standing next to a highway with cars whizzing by, some gas-station sign showing a price of $3.159, a boring economist opining on supply and demand, and gas pumping into a car's tank—will be Everyman commenting on his plight.

"These gas prices are so high, I can't afford it anymore," laments Everyman.

As he willingly pumps that $3 per gallon gas right into his car.

And just as willingly sips on a half-liter bottle of water that cost him a buck inside the convenience store—or about $8 per gallon.

12. IS MASSACHUSETTS
A FAMILY-FRIENDLY STATE?

William V. D'Antonio was ticked.

During the 2004 presidential campaign, he kept hearing Republicans lambaste "Massachusetts liberals" as the enemies of family values. The previous fall, the Bay State's Supreme Judicial Court had ruled that gay couples had the right to marry. In the eyes of some conservatives, that one decision transformed the state into a toxic waste dump of liberalism, out to ruin the American family. It was as if people from Massachusetts had some kind of disease and the cure was family values, straight from the Bible Belt.

So D'Antonio, a retired sociology professor, decided to do a little research. What he found was rather shocking. When it came to family values, the Bay State beat the Bible Belt hands down.

Take teen pregnancy. Teenagers from Texas get pregnant nearly twice as often as Massachusetts teens. Massachusetts also has a lower divorce rate than Texas, or any other Bible Belt state. D'Antonio found that Alabama, Arkansas, Arizona, Florida, Georgia, Mississippi, North Carolina, Oklahoma, South Carolina, and Texas had some of the highest divorce rates in the country. "By comparison," he wrote in an op-ed piece called "Walking the Walk on Family Values," "nine states in the Northeast were among those with the lowest divorce rates: Connecticut, Massachusetts, Maine, New Hampshire, New Jersey, New York,

Pennsylvania, Rhode Island, and Vermont."

There's more bad news for Bible Belt states. Almost a quarter of Texas high school students drop out—again, nearly double the rate in Massachusetts. Other southern states also have high dropout rates. Additionally, because those Bay State teens stay in high school, they're more likely to build the human capital needed to succeed in life. And they are better off when they go to work, so they make more money to take care of their families.

"The liberals from Massachusetts have long prided themselves on their emphasis on education, and it has paid off," D'Antonio wrote. "People who stay in school longer get married at a later age, when they are more mature, are more likely to secure a better job, and job income increases with each level of formal education."

So while Bible Belt Republicans talked the talk on family values, D'Antonio argues, the folks in Massachusetts walked the walk. "By their behavior you can know them as the true conservatives," D'Antonio concluded. "They are showing how to conserve family life through the way they live their family values."

A Ring of Gold

There is at least one place where Bay Staters and Bible Belters do agree. And that's on the importance of marriage. God said that it was not good for men—or for women—to be alone. And it turns out to be true—by almost every measure imaginable.

As University of Chicago sociology professor Linda Waite and journalist Maggie Gallagher put it in their book *The Case for Marriage*, tying the knot has physical, material, and spiritual benefits. "Married people live longer," they wrote, "have better health, earn more money and accumulate more wealth, feel more fulfilled in their lives, enjoy more satisfying sexual relationships, and have happier and more successful children than those who remain single, cohabit, or get divorced."

In a study published in 2002, British economists Andrew Oswald and Jonathan Gardner of England's Warwick University found that marriage might even help keep you alive. They discovered that, over a seven-year period, a married man was 9 percent less likely to die than a single man. For men, being single was a worse health risk than smoking. (Oswald, tongue in cheek, urged all male smokers to rush out and get married.)

The economists even found that being married was better than being rich. "Forget cash," Oswald told the BBC. "It is as clear as day from the data that marriage, rather than money, is what keeps people alive. It makes perfect sense to ask how a ring of gold can possibly do this. But the honest answer is: we just don't know."

In his book *Imagine! A God Blessed America*, Richard Land, president of the Southern Baptist Ethics and Religious Liberty Commission, claims that marriage may even be a miracle cure for poverty. "The one thing that would lift more people out of poverty than any other single factor is for women to be married—and stay married—to the father of their children," he wrote. "Divorce would shrink to a rare phenomenon. The vast majority of children would be once again reared in intact families."

The 2006 "State of Our Unions" report from the Institute on Marriage at Rutgers University made nearly the same point about the economic power of marriage. "Marriage is a wealth generating institution," Institute director Barbara Dafoe Whitehead wrote. "Married couples create more economic assets on average than do otherwise similar singles or cohabiting couples." Then she added, "Compared to those continuously married, those who never married have a reduction in wealth of 75 percent and those who divorced and didn't remarry have a reduction of 73 percent."

In an interview for the PBS series *Frontline*, Whitehead argued that too often marriage is thought of as a strictly private affair. This ignores the broader social impact of marriage. "We don't like to think of it this way, but marriage is an institution that covers more than just the private intimate sexual and romantic relationships between two freely consenting adults," she said.

> Marriage is a primary social institution for rearing children. To have that change, and change so dramatically in a very short period of time, obviously has big effects. It has effects on kids. It has effects on adults. But those effects fall disproportionately on children and on the poor. So that's why I'm concerned about it, because there is a dramatic impact and measurable impact on the lives of children.

A Cord of Three Strands

How does marriage accomplish all this? For one thing, married couples pool their income and can live cheaper together than apart. Because of their long-term commitment, each partner has a safety net, someone to rely on if things go wrong.

Spouses also protect each other from risk—whether in the area of health, finances, or anything else. "If you think of the Christian marriage vow—in sickness and in health—it seems that people will stay together even if one gets M.S. or cancer or gets disabled," Linda Waite told the Catholic journal *America*. "It's insurance, and insurance is expensive. Emotionally, it's important in that if you get sick, there's someone who will take care of you."

That kind of partnership is reflected in Ecclesiastes 4:9–12, a Scripture passage often used in Christian weddings:

> Two are better than one, because they have a good return for their work: If one falls down, his friend can help him up. But pity the man who falls and has no one to help him up! Also, if two lie down together, they will keep warm. But how can one keep warm

alone? Though one may be overpowered, two can defend themselves. A cord of three strands is not quickly broken.

Married couples also take advantage of one of the most basic economic principles of all—specialization. Each spouse focuses on those areas in which they excel and, working together, accomplish more than they can apart. One keeps the family checkbook, washes clothes, and fixes leaky faucets; the other takes care of car maintenance, cooking, and housecleaning, for example.

In marriage, Linda Waite told *America*, "You can say, I like to cook and you like to clean, and I'll get to be a terrific cook because I'll never have to clean. Two people together produce more. They can have a high quality life because they have two specialists, whereas people who live alone don't specialize."

Three strands make a cord strong, and these three strands— more wealth, insurance against risk, and specialization—make a marriage strong.

A Husband and a Job

There's one other area where couples can improve their economic circumstances by specializing. If one spouse needs to get additional training, or go back to college or grad school to improve their job prospects, being married gives them the support needed to accomplish that goal.

That's what Angela Whitiker discovered in her long journey out of poverty.

In the early 1990s, Whitiker faced insurmountable odds. She had grown up in a broken home and had met her father only once when she was ten. Smelling of whiskey, he showed up at Angela's mother's house just long enough to promise to buy her a bicycle—a promise he never kept—before disappearing again for good.

"Within a few years," according to a *New York Times* profile, "she was using men as a substitute for her father and her adolescent longing for him."

By fifteen, she was pregnant with her first child. By twenty-three, she was the mother of five children, had been married and separated, and been a casualty of the crack epidemic of the 1980's. She had lost and would later win back custody of her children, and had worked a variety of odd jobs, from sausage vendor to picking butter beans.

In 1993, when *Times* reporter Isabel Wilkerson first met Whitiker, she was living in an impoverished neighborhood of Englewood in Chicago, and was caught up in a daily struggle to get by. "For her," Wilkerson wrote, "each day meant trying to piece together enough to take care of herself and her kids—one day petitioning the fathers for child support, the next counting what was left of her food stamps; one minute rushing to an administrator's office to get bus vouchers for school, the next bargaining with the electric company to get her lights turned back on."

> To keep her family out of the projects and on what might be described as the upper rung of poverty, she had taken up with a man who worked handling baggage at O'Hare International Airport. He paid the rent and was the father of her fifth child, Johnathan. His paycheck gave her breathing room to get into a pre-nursing program at Kennedy-King Community College on the South Side.

But Whitiker's relationship with Jonathan's father fell apart, and she had to drop out of school, leaving her once again trapped in poverty. Although *Times* readers, having heard of Whitiker's plight, had responded generously and sent donations to help her out, that charity couldn't help in the long haul. She lacked the human capital—the education, the motivation, and other spiritual assets—needed to transform her life. She was still, in Wilkerson's words, "a single mother with only a high school equivalency degree, no career skills, no assets and no immediate prospects for independence."

With no other options, Whitiker moved her family to the Robert Taylor Homes. A gang-infested public-housing project, it was one of the most dangerous places in the city of Chicago. Wilkerson described Whitiker's new life in heartbreaking detail. She and her five kids lived in "an urban no-man's land where you could move about only when the gangs that ran the place let you. The elevators, sticky with urine, didn't work, and gunshots were background music."

"From the start," Wilkerson reported, "Ms. Whitiker felt that it was beneath her."

> She looked down on the women who had grown accustomed to bullet holes over their dinette tables, who watched "All My Children" and ate Doritos all day and didn't seem to want anything better. She carried the gun to protect herself and had to use it once when, having climbed nine flights of stairs, she found some strangers playing cards at her kitchen table. She fired shots into the ceiling to get them out.
>
> It was the lowest rung of the poverty class in America, lower in a way than the worst nights in a crack house in her early 20's, because now she was fully conscious of exactly where she was.

Whitiker bounced between a few minimum-wage jobs, working at a fast-food restaurant and taking a second job as a security guard. But she was going nowhere fast.

Then Whitiker met Vincent Allen. He was a police detective who also moonlighted as a security officer. Not long afterwards, Whitiker moved from the projects into Allen's home. After they had settled in together, Allen encouraged Whitiker to go back to school. Not only that, but he paid the bills, watched the kids, and kept their house running while she studied.

Over the next six years, Whitiker earned a degree in nursing. It was a long, uphill climb. She had never been a good student, and had to work harder and longer than her classmates. But she made it. She graduated and then, in 2001, passed her state boards. With a new job as a nurse at a nearby hospital, Angela Whitiker had finally arrived. Soon afterwards, she and Allen were married.

Even after all that, life wasn't perfect for Whitiker. The long climb up had taken a toll on her children. Her son Nicholas, who had been the man of the house since he was ten, got involved in a gang. Another son was shot by a gang member and, while he recovered, seemed lost to the streets. Whitiker's other children are doing well in school and plan on going to college. And Whitiker told Wilkerson that she hadn't lost hope for her older sons.

"Can't you see your life is going down the drain, and you're the only one who can save it?" she asks her sons. "You want a quick way out. There is no quick way out. I tried that. It doesn't work." Then she told Wilkerson, "I'm a late bloomer, and I know it's not too late for them."

Why Don't They Just Get Married?

If marriage is an economic miracle cure, then why doesn't everyone tie the knot? The reason is that marriage is hard. As Whitiker told her sons, there are no shortcuts.

Andrew Oswald, an economics professor at the University of Warwick, points out that the economic benefits of marriage take a long time to build up. In an essay called "The Extraordinary Effects of Marriage," Oswald noted that "if you study people in their early 20s, then those who are married barely earn more than singles. It appears that the 'marriage wage premium,' as it is sometimes called by researchers, actually gets stronger through time as the years pass and the marriage gets longer."

Then there's the marriage-partner problem. One of the keys to Angela Whitiker's success was the man she eventually married. Vincent Allen was college-educated and had a good job. He had some human capital—and financial capital—to work with. When in her younger years she had married someone with fewer prospects, things turned out a lot differently. As economist and author Julianne Malveaux told NPR, "When two broke folk get together, problems don't divide, they multiply."

Barbara Ehrenreich, author of *Nickel and Dimed: On (Not) Getting By in America*, also noted that marriage doesn't work for everyone. In a few cases, money can trap people in unhealthy relationships. While working on *Nickel and Dimed*, Ehrenreich met a woman who was trapped in an abusive relationship and couldn't afford to get out. "She wanted to leave him, and had tried it once, but the hard fact was that she and the two children could not survive on her $10 an hour clerical job," Ehrenreich wrote on her blog. "He was no winner, but his $11 an hour contribution to the household made him, tragically, a keeper."

There are signs that the gaps in human capital between rich and poor—which have a dramatic effect on incomes—are also affecting marriage. As *The Economist* reported in a story titled "Marriage in America: The Frayed Knot," the divorce rates of college-educated couples have been dropping for decades, while divorce has been growing more common among the less-educated.

"Only 4% of the children of mothers with college degrees are born out of wedlock," *The Economist* reported. "And the divorce rate among college-educated women has plummeted. Of those who first tied the knot between 1975 and 1979, 29% were divorced within ten years. Among those who first married between 1990 and 1994, only 16.5% were."

Things were almost the exact opposite for less-educated couples. "Among high school dropouts, the divorce rate rose from 38% for those who first married in 1975–79 to 46% for those who first married in 1990–94," according to *The Economist.* "Among those with a high school diploma but no college, it rose from 35% to 38%. And these figures are only part of the story. Many mothers avoid divorce by never marrying in the first place. The out-of-wedlock birth rate among women who drop out of high school is 15%. Among African-Americans, it is a staggering 67%."

All of this is leading to something resembling a caste system, Kay Hymowitz of the Manhattan Institute, a conservative think tank, told *The Economist.* Hymowitz is author of *Marriage and Caste,* which argues that "middle-class kids growing up with two biological parents are 'socialised for success.'"

> They do better in school, get better jobs and go on to create intact families of their own. Children of single parents or broken families do worse in school, get worse jobs and go on to have children out of wedlock. This makes it more likely that those born near the top or the bottom will stay where they started.

According to *The Economist,* this leads to "a nation of separate and unequal families."

Living Together

Ironically, one of the strategies that some couples thought would strengthen their marriages ended up weakening them. In recent years, the number of Americans living together before marriage has risen dramatically. The idea is to have a trial run at marriage before making a long-term commitment. But people living together miss out on one of the prime economic benefits of marriage. They don't specialize. Instead, they become "intimate strangers," as one study put it. They live together but pursue individual agendas.

It's a lack of commitment that keeps them from specializing. As economists Shelley Lundberg and Robert Pollak explained, specializing only pays off if the relationship lasts. If the commitment isn't there up front, it's risky to do the more intensive and narrower investment of time and effort characteristic of specialization. So people specialize less—they remain intimate strangers. Then, their relationship is less valuable because they aren't specializing. It's a vicious cycle—low commitment deters specialization, which reduces commitment, and so on.

According to the Marriage Institute at Rutgers University, cohabitation is correlated with three other major consequences:

- A higher rate of divorce for couples that go on to get married.

- More domestic violence toward women and physical and sexual abuse of children.

- Lower levels of happiness and well-being than married couples.

"Despite its widespread acceptance by the young, the remarkable growth of unmarried cohabitation in recent years does not appear to be in children's or the society's best interest," David Popenoe and Barbara Dafoe Whitehead wrote in *Should We Live Together? What Young Adults Need to Know about Cohabitation before Marriage.*

The evidence suggests that it has weakened marriage and the intact, two-parent family and thereby damaged our social well-being, especially that of women and children. We cannot go back in history, but it seems time to establish some guidelines for the practice of cohabitation and to seriously question the further institutionalization of this new family form.

Massachusetts Is Family-Friendly

What about William D'Antonio? Is there any systematic way of assessing whether he's right? Is Massachusetts a family-friendly state? To help answer these questions, we put together our own "Family-Friendly Index" and ranked all fifty states plus the District of Columbia. We didn't do any rigorous statistical testing of the index, but it still can tell us something about the state of the American family.

Our index is based on statewide statistics on marriage and divorce, educational quality, teen pregnancies and teen abortions, housing costs, household incomes, and church membership. The things that strengthen families make the value of the index go up, and vice versa. What we found is in table 12.1.

The upper Midwest has the most family-friendly states, while Massachusetts comes in fifth. The Bay State has a low divorce rate and is ranked high on education, income levels, and church membership (Massachusetts has a lot of Roman Catholics). Western states (except Utah) fared poorly, with most having high housing costs and low church-membership rates. The Bible Belt states

TABLE 12.1	MOST AND LEAST FAMILY-FRIENDLY STATES		
Ten Best		**Ten Worst**	
Rank	**State**	**Rank**	**State**
1.	North Dakota	51.	District of Columbia
2.	Utah	50.	Nevada
3.	South Dakota	49.	Hawaii
4.	Minnesota	48.	Florida
5.	Massachusetts	47.	California
6.	Wisconsin	46.	Oregon
7.	Iowa	45.	Arizona
8.	Nebraska	44.	New Mexico
9.	Pennsylvania	43.	Washington
10.	New Hampshire	42.	West Virginia

Source: Authors' calculations based on various publicly available data.

were mostly in the middle of the pack—they certainly did not rise to the top.

The Bible encourages strong and healthy families to help with our overall spiritual well-being. Of course, there are such families everywhere, but some places seem to make it easier than others.

It turns out that Bible Belt states have some work to do before they are really family-friendly.

It is definitely true that married people are much better off than single or divorced people along many dimensions. That doesn't mean, however, that poor people would be just fine if only they would get married. Marriage probably isn't a direct cause of higher incomes and better mental and physical health. Instead, the sorts of people who are capable of committing to a strong marriage are also the sort of people who earn more, are emotionally balanced, and so on. How did they get to be that type of person?

By developing spiritual assets and human capital, which as we've already seen, are the same things that help lift people out of poverty. Married people are less likely to be poor because they have the spiritual assets and human capital that help them succeed in marriage and in life.

EPILOGUE
THE PARABLE OF
THE GOOD ECONOMIST

In the tenth chapter of Luke, Jesus tells one of his most famous parables:

A man was going down from Jerusalem to Jericho, when he fell into the hands of robbers. They stripped him of his clothes, beat him and went away, leaving him half dead. A priest happened to be going down the same road, and when he saw the man, he passed by on the other side. So too, a Levite, when he came to the place and saw him, passed by on the other side. But a Samaritan, as he traveled, came where the man was; and when he saw him, he took pity on him. He went to him and bandaged his wounds, pouring on oil and wine. Then he put the man on his own donkey, took him to an inn and took care of him. The next day he took out two silver coins and gave them to the innkeeper. "Look after him," he said, "and when I return, I will reimburse you for any extra expense you may have." (Luke 10:30–34)

The point seems obvious, at least to modern readers. The priest and the Levite were heartless, self-centered religious hypocrites who claimed to love God but couldn't care less about their fellow man. The Samaritan, despite being an outcast, showed that he really loved God by loving his neighbor.

Convinced that we already know the answer, we rarely ask an obvious question: "Why did the priest and the Levite pass by on the other side?"

New Testament scholar Scot McKnight takes on that question in his book *The Jesus Creed.* The answer is surprising. The priest and the Levite were not hypocrites or cruel, heartless, and uncaring. Instead, they were doing the right thing. They had good intentions. Not only that, McKnight says, anyone who heard Jesus tell this parable would have also thought that they did the right thing.

Why? Because priests and Levites were forbidden to touch dead bodies—because touching a corpse would have made them unclean, or sinful, in God's eyes. At first sight, the wounded man would have looked like a dead body, and by law, they were supposed to avoid a corpse. And even if the wounded traveler was only near death, they couldn't risk getting too close. If he died, they would be tainted by sin. So they did the ritually correct thing and passed by on the other side. The priest and the Levite thought they were obeying the Bible's commands, and in so doing would earn God's favor. They had good intentions but never thought through the consequences of their actions.

The Samaritan, on the other hand, looked at the wounded man from a different point of view. His first concern was not for his own religious purity. Instead, he worried first about the fate of the wounded man. The Samaritan examined the man's wounds, applied the first century's version of first aid, and went out of his way to make sure that the wounded man was well cared for. He had good intentions and followed up those intentions with actions that led to the wounded man's recovery.

At the end of the parable, Jesus asked, "Which of these three do you think was a neighbor to the man who fell into the hands of robbers?" A teacher of the law, who had earlier challenged Jesus, replied, "The one who had mercy on him." So Jesus told him, "Go and do likewise."

Some of the conclusions we've found in *Good Intentions* seem somehow wrong. Take the minimum wage. Raising it feels like a good idea that would have "a powerful moral and political impact," as former Labor Secretary Robert Reich points out. But it doesn't work nearly as well, when it comes to helping poor families, as the Earned Income Tax Credit (EITC). Nobody holds rallies or organizes national campaigns to raise the EITC, but perhaps we should.

What about Wal-Mart? Not long after Muhammad Yunus and the Grameen Bank of Bangladesh won the 2006 Nobel Peace Prize, John Tierney, a *New York Times* columnist, wondered if Sam Walton deserved one as well. Tierney's column sparked an angry barrage of letters. We're not about to nominate Walton for a Nobel, but Tierney makes a good point. "Has any organization in the world lifted more people out of poverty than Wal-Mart?" he asked. The numbers seem to back him up. In 1981, more than 795 million people in China, or 57.7 percent of the population, lived in extreme poverty—on less than a dollar a day. By 2001, that number had dropped by more than five hundred million people. One of the major reasons is that millions of formerly poor Chinese peasants now work in factories making products for America. For them, extreme poverty has become history.

One thing does seem clear. Buying a $15 Wal-Mart bra may never feel as moral as buying a $30 "justice bra," but it may do more to help poor garment workers in China—just as making greed green by selling pollution credits may do more to save the environment than buying carbon offsets.

Mrs. Williams' Legacy

On a Sunday morning in July 2007, a small group of people gathered around a long table in the pastor's office at Oakdale Covenant Church in Chicago to pay tribute to Delories Williams. There were a few tears, especially when Sethras Jones spoke of her long friendship with Mrs. Williams, how the two had been closer than sisters. But most of the time, there was laughter—especially from the six young college students sitting around the table. Jessica Motley and Jovanne Hughes told of their camping adventures with Mrs. Williams, who had been their Girl Scout leader from Brownies to Cadets.

"Mrs. Williams did not play," Hughes said, laughing about her mentor's no-nonsense approach, even on camping trips. Then one of the students told of how, when she needed a letter of reference, Mrs. Williams detailed every community project the student had ever done. And how each spring, right around finals, Mrs. Williams arranged for care packages full of home-made cakes and cookies to be sent to every student from the church. Another student told of how she had never imagined leaving Chicago and going to college until Mrs. Williams had taken her on a college tour.

As the students spoke, the seven volunteers around the table beamed with delight. Their smiles widened when Daniel King, who had just completed his masters in accounting, talked about inspiring younger generations of students to go to college. King recalled how, when another Oakdale student graduated with an accounting degree, he had told recruiters from his firm to keep an eye out for her. (She got a job with the firm—not because of his recommendation—but because she was an outstanding student.)

More than thirty years ago, Rev. Willie Jemmison, the former pastor of Oakdale, gave Mrs. Williams and her friends a challenge—to get all of the church's children into college. The task seemed overwhelming. Oakdale is in a poor, predominantly African-American community—where prospects are slim, schools struggle, and few kids go to college. But Mrs. Williams had a job to do, and she would not let anything—not even cancer—get in her way. She and the host of volunteers from the Academic Excellence ministry did whatever it took to help their children succeed. If a student needed tutoring, they found a tutor. When they realized their students needed help filling out financial-aid forms or college applications, the volunteers became experts in navigating the application process. And if a child needed a second chance, Mrs. Williams made sure they got it—then she kept a watchful eye on them to make sure they didn't waste it. The only measure that mattered was a diploma. Mrs. Williams and the other volunteers would not rest until their good intentions had become reality.

Go and do likewise.

ACKNOWLEDGMENTS

Thanks to everyone at Moody, especially Betsey Newenhuyse, who first dreamed up this book, and to Andy McGuire, for helping us bring the book to life.

From Bob Smietana:

Thanks to Pastor Griffin, Sethras Jones, Regina Williams, and all the volunteers in the Academic Excellence Ministry at Oakdale Covenant Church in Chicago; to Dick and Judy Johnson for your insights on global poverty and economic development; to Wendy Lawton, a great agent; to the North Park Friends group; to the Smietana and Gaulke families for your love and support; and to Kathy, Sophie, Eli, and Marel, for making me the richest (and luckiest man in the world).

From Chuck North:

I thank Tom Odegaard for many hours of helpful conversation on issues related to poverty and economic development. His ideas and knowledge were a great benefit to me both before and during the process of writing this book, and many of the ideas in this book have their origin in my discussions with him. I also thank Tisha Emerson for her insights on matters relating to environmental economics. Overall, I thank all of my colleagues in the Department of Economics at Baylor University for providing a thought-provoking and intellectually stimulating environment in which Christian economists can contemplate how their faith should affect and enlighten their approaches to the profession of economics. Thanks also to Wendy Lawton for picking up a stray client.

For further reading and a complete bibliography,
please visit
www.GoodIntentionsBook.com.